CHILDREN OF POVERTY

Studies on the Effects of Single Parenthood, the Feminization of Poverty, and Homelessness

edited by

STUART BRUCHEY
University of Maine

A GARLAND SERIES

CHILD ABUSE REPORTING

An Urban Profile

ANTOINETTE A. COLEMAN

GARLAND PUBLISHING, Inc.
New York & London / 1995

Library of Congress Cataloging-in-Publication Data

Coleman, Antoinette A., 1956–
    Child abuse reporting : an urban profile / Antoinette A.
Coleman.
        p.   cm. — (Children of poverty)
    Includes bibliographical references and index.
    ISBN 0-8153-2194-5 (alk. paper)
    1. Child abuse—Reporting—United States. 2. Child wel-
fare—United States. I. Title. II. Series.
HV8079.C46C65 1995
362.76'63'0973—dc20   95-38866

Printed on acid-free, 250-year-life paper
Manufactured in the United States of America

To my mother, Ethel Beckett Coleman, and sister-in-law, Aloma Thompson Beckett, who helped me realize the rewards of perseverance.

Contents

Illustrations

FIGURES

TABLES

TABLES (cont.)

MAP

Preface

Understanding the dynamics of child abuse reporting is essential to intervene effectively with children and their families suspected of child maltreatment (abuse). Since the inception of state reporting laws mandated by the 1974 Child Abuse Prevention and Treatment Act, child abuse reporting has dramatically increased over the years. This increase in reporting has sparked the interest and concern of child welfare practitioners and other professionals. Members of the professional community responsible for the well-being of children and families and some lay persons have begun to question the current reporting trends and report investigation dispositions rendered to alleged reports of child abuse.

Such attention has influenced a few researchers to examine the phenomena of child abuse reporting. The literature on child abuse reporting is still, however, quite scant. It consists of some National Incidence Studies that produce statistics on reports received by states, children reported for suspected maltreatment, type of individuals/agencies making reports, and report substantiation rates. But, for the most part, empirical studies that venture beyond statistical accounting of reports are limited. Much of the literature in the field of child maltreatment has focused on the etiology of child abuse as it relates to the culture of poverty, cultural and individual deviance, types of abuse, and victims of child abuse, just to name a few. This trend in the literature suggests a need for increased attention into examining the content of child abuse reports and the types of report dispositions investigative agencies are able to render.

In an effort to broaden our knowledge of child maltreatment, the central issue of this book is on child abuse reporting in an urban area. The book examines child abuse reporting from the aspect of reporters of abuse, the reporting sources. Using an ecological perspective, the book examines the characteristics of reported children and their families and the investigative dispositions of child abuse reports generated by two groups of urban reporting sources: medical and non-medical reporters.

Urban medical reporting sources of child abuse studied in this book are professional health care staff (physicians, nurses, social workers, therapists, technicians, etc.) employed at inner-city acute, chronic, and mental hospitals as well as their out-patient clinics; family planning clinics; well baby clinics; private health practitioners' offices; and local and state health departments. Urban non-medical reporting sources of child abuse are personnel of inner-city public social services agencies, private social services agencies, public housing authorities, schools, child care facilities, law enforcement agencies, juvenile services agencies; and neighbors, friends, victims, relatives. biological/adoptive parents, foster parents, stepparents, and anonymous callers.

This study on urban child abuse reporting delineates the different characteristics medical and non-medical reporters identify as incidents of child abuse in their reports, and the types of report disposition associated with reports from each of these reporting sources. Specifically , the study examines 1) the characteristics of the reported children (age, race, and gender) and their families, 2) type of alleged abuse (physical or sexual), 3) severity of alleged abuse, 4) alleged perpetrators, and 5) socioeconomic status of the family's area of residence (poverty or non-poverty areas). Furthermore, the study looks at child abuse report dispositions by using the categories of substantiated (abuse confirmed) and unsubstantiated (abuse not confirmed). The correlation of report characteristics and report dispositions with reporting sources make this study unique.

This book attempts to fulfill two needs through the findings of this study on urban child abuse reporting. First, the critical need for more theoretical examination into the area of child abuse reporting. The importance of further theoretical examination into this area of child maltreatment helps to expand existing conceptual models, and develop new frameworks to explain how various individuals and systems determine what is or is not child abuse. And second, the need to advance practical knowledge and application for reporters of abuse and practitioners responsible for investigating alleged reports and providing intervention to at risk families. Such practical knowledge and application helps child protective services practitioners better understand the strengths and weakness of different child abuse reporters. This information also affords child welfare practitioners, administrators and policy-makers a stronger foundation for establishing innovative programs directed at strengthening the knowledge gaps among reporters of child abuse to help reduce unfounded reports. Furthermore, the advancement of practical knowledge and application can help to reduce some of the ambivalence in the child welfare system that practitioners face in rendering a report confirmed (substantiated) or not confirmed (unsubstantiated) for abuse.

This book is divided into two parts. Part One of this book, Chapters 1, 2 and 3 respectively, present an introduction, review of the literature and conceptual framework of child abuse reporting. Part Two, Chapters 4, 5, 6, discuss the research methodology, sample, and findings for this study on urban child abuse reporting. And, Chapter 7 offers discussion and research and practice implications.

Acknowledgments

Many people have played a role in making this book possible. Special thanks to Malinda Orlin for her untiringly direction; Ruth Young, Oliver Harris, and William Bechill of the University of Maryland at Baltimore School of Social Work for their many hours spent reviewing the research for this book; Henry Brehm of the University of Maryland Baltimore County Department of Sociology for his statistical expertise; and Carolyn Finney of the Woodbourne Children's Diagnostic and Treatment Center Inc, Baltimore, Maryland for her professional knowledge and experiences in working with abused children; and Tracy Modlin, Yolando Lowery, Ronald Taylor and Craig Gotschall who served as research assistance.

I want to especially acknowledge and express my thanks to Anthony E. Fairfax for his technical assistance in helping me complete this book; Catherine Born, Lily Gold, Catherine Nelson and Charlotte Johnson for their encouragement and insights.

Last but not least, Harold E. Russell, III, and my family who have supported my endeavors for many years to achieve this goal.

A. A. C.

Child Abuse Reporting

Part One

Overview

I

Introduction and Study Overview

Child abuse has become an increasingly visible contemporary social problem. In recent years significant public resources have been directed toward alerting communities to the problem of child abuse and the importance of reporting suspected maltreatment of children. Today all fifty states, the District of Columbia, and Virgin Islands have child abuse reporting laws (Reiniger, Robinson, McHugh 1995). These laws usually mandate reporting for certain professionals and encourage reporting by others.

Many landmark events in history paved the road to the enactment of laws mandating the reporting of suspected child abuse. One of the most notable events leading to the reporting of child maltreatment was the 1874 case of Mary Ellen, a severely abused child who was tied to a bed, whipped, and stabbed with scissors (Karger and Stoesz 1994). The abuse of Mary Ellen was brought to the attention of the New York Society for the Prevention of Cruelty to Animals to intervene on her behalf (339). In 1875 the New York Society for the Prevention of Cruelty to Children (NYSPCC) was established (Reiniger, Robinson, and McHugh 1995). The NYSPCC was the first child protective services agency in the world (64). The federal government and states did not, however, begin to take a serious look at child maltreatment and the need for mandatory reporting until 1962, when Dr. Henry Kempe and his colleagues publicized "The Battered Child Syndrome" (64).

Even with the devastating and traumatic cases of child maltreatment validation by Dr. Kempe in the early 1960s, no federal legislation for mandatory reporting of child abuse and neglect was enacted during this period. It was not until 1974, more than a decade later, that the United States Congress enacted the Child Abuse Prevention and Treatment Act. The 1974 Child Abuse Prevention and Treatment Act required states to adopt

3

mandatory reporting laws. This legislation worked to change child abuse and neglect from a *private trouble*, not requiring societal intervention, to a major social *public issue*.

CHILD ABUSE REPORTERS

Originally reporting laws were established primarily for physicians. These reporting laws required physicians to report *serious physical injuries* or *non-accidental injuries*. Physicians were seen as the most likely professionals to see abused and neglected children and as those with the greatest degree of expertise to diagnose the signs and symptoms of child maltreatment (Besharov 1990). For many physicians, their reporting of child maltreatment was often limited to the most serious cases of physical injury or health conditions resulting from abuse or neglect. It was later recognized that while physicians are key reporters of abuse, they represented only one source of reporters.

Reporting laws progressed as the problem of child maltreatment became more evident. The laws began to recognize that all professionals responsible for the care of children should be mandated to report suspected maltreatment. Today numerous medical and non-medical professionals who serve children are required to report. In all states those professionals required to report are physicians, nurses, emergency room personnel, coroners and medical examiners, dentists, mental health professionals (psychologists or therapists), social workers, teachers and other school officials, day care or child care workers, and law enforcement personnel. In some states pharmacists, foster parents, clergy, attorneys, day care licensing inspectors, film or photo processors (to detect sexual exploitation cases), substance abuse counselors, camp counselors and staff, family mediators, child abuse information and referral staff and volunteers, and Christian Science practitioners are required to report (24).

Professionals mandated by law who fail to report suspected incidents of maltreatment in almost every state are often subject to significant penalty if they fail to do so. Penalties for mandated reporters who fail to report in many states consist of endangerment of their licenses to practice or criminal penalties. Criminal penalties are often at the misdemeanor level including fines of $100 to $1,000, five days to one year in jail, or both (37).

To encourage public reporting in most states a good faith reporter may not be prosecuted. For reports made maliciously, out of personal prejudices, or by professionals who purposefully bias information for their own gain, there is no immunity. Such behavior on the part of reporters nullify the presumption of good faith reporting. Direct evidence of bad faith reporting is not often found (Besharov 1990).

STATISTICS ON CHILD
MALTREATMENT REPORTING

The enactment of the 1974 Child Abuse Prevention and Treatment Act not only expanded those individuals mandated to report, but it also led to a dramatic increase in the number of children reported for abuse and neglect. To illustrate, 669,000 reports were received nationwide in 1976 (American Humane Association 1978). Between 1980 and 1986, see Figure 1.1, the number of reported cases increased 66 percent (Besharov 1990; Burnley 1986). By 1987, 2,178,000 children were reported for abuse and neglect, in 1990 2.7 million were reported, and 2.9 million were reported in 1993 (Reiniger, Robinson, and McHugh 1995).

From 1976 to 1992 the overall number of children reported for suspected child maltreatment increased yearly. It was not until 1993 that the rate of reporting did not increase. In 1993 the reporting rate was slightly under 43 per 1,000 children 17 years and younger (U.S. Department of Health and Human Services 1995). The overall reporting rate from 1976 to 1993 showed a 331 percent increase for this eighteen year period (2-2).

Fluctuations have occurred over the years in reporting. To illustrate, the average annual growth rate in reporting for 1976 to 1983 was 9 percent, 7 percent for 1984 to 1988, and approximately 3 percent for 1989 to 1993 (U.S. Department of Health and Human Services 1995). It is apparent that the percentage of yearly increase declined over the years, but the *total* number of children reported for suspected maltreatment continued to increase until 1993.

Figure 1.1

1980-1986 Child Maltreatment Reporting

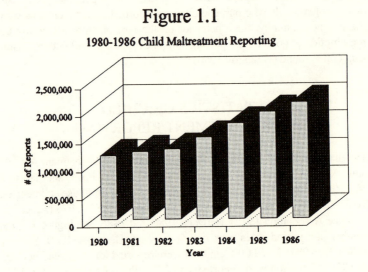

Source: American Humane Association, 1987

ISSUES IN REPORTING

Child abuse reporting over the years has not been without its controversies. Many debates have taken place among professionals and other concerned citizens regarding reporting obligations, legal protection for reporters, and the legal definitions of child maltreatment, particularly abuse, just to name a few.

Child abuse reporting rates are becoming a major issue of concern among child welfare professionals. These professionals are beginning to closely scrutinize child maltreatment reporting rates to determine the various trends in reporting, and the impact increased reporting is having on the child welfare service delivery system.

Despite the overall trends upward in the number of reports, there have been fluctuations. For example during 1986 it was estimated that 1.6 million children were reported nationwide for maltreatment, down from the 1.9

million reported in 1985 (Besharov 1990; Maryland Department of Human Resources 1989). These changes in reporting sparked the question—was there less maltreatment? Most child welfare professionals doubted there was less maltreatment. Many postulated that such occurrences could, indeed, be a result of distortions in the reporting process.

Closer examination suggests that fluctuations in reporting do not always denote less maltreatment. Studies examining the trends in reporting rates indicate a vast number of recognizably endangered children still are not being reported to authorities (Reiniger, Robinson, and McHugh 1995). Many of these unreported cases are children who are known to individuals who can help them. Unfortunately, these children go unreported because some professionals are failing to report even when they suspect maltreatment (Besharov 1990). A national incidence study conducted by the United States Department of Health and Human Services (1988) indicated professionals were not reporting almost half the maltreated children they encountered.

Further research by Sedlak (1989) in 1986 indicated professionals failed to report 30 percent of the children they encountered who were seriously physically abused, 50 percent of those moderately physically abused, and almost 40 percent of those sexually abused. The failure to report is even greater with neglect. Professionals failed to report about 70 percent of the seriously physically neglected cases and three-quarters of the moderately physically neglected cases they saw. These percentages indicate, as illustrated in Figure 1.2, an estimated total number of 60,000 children with obvious physical injuries who warranted hospitalization, almost 184,000 moderately physically injured children, and about 50,000 sexually abused children that went unreported (Besharov 1990). Such findings are not only astounding, but suggest many children who could be helped are still at risk of being seriously maltreated or killed.

There are several possible reasons for such reporting behaviors on the part of some professionals who fail to report:

1 lack of clarity regarding the designated authority to receive reports;
2. lack of understanding on their part as to what constitutes a suspected child maltreatment incident when serious injury may not be present;
3. a reluctance to report because of lengthy court proceedings and/or fear of repercussions; and

4. the belief that they can best help the family to resolve the problem (Children's Defense Fund 1989).

Such explanations suggest more attention must be directed toward understanding the reporting behaviors of reporters and any other gaps that exist in the system.

Figure 1.2

Under Reporting

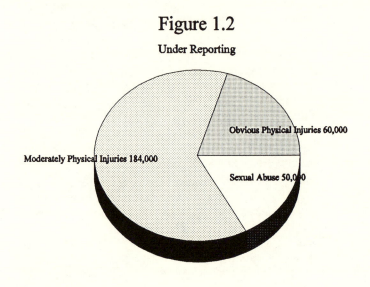

Source: Besharov, 1990

Further examination into fluctuations in reporting suggest such occurrences may be attributed to the difficulties that exist in our system to document accurately incidents of child maltreatment. Fluctuations in the number of suspected cases reported is but one example of the difficulty that policy makers and researchers face when forced to take an entirely separate action—making the report—as an indicator of the extent of a different phenomenon, the maltreatment. Despite the many conceptual and practical difficulties equated with reporting incidents of child maltreatment, reporting is still our best marker for reaching children at risk of maltreatment.

Trends in reporting have not only raised the important and timely questions about reporters, but they have impacted greatly on resources in the child welfare delivery system. Specifically, increased reporting has inundated the already scant resources of child protective service agencies. Child welfare workers, particularly child protective services (CPS) workers, are overwhelmed with the escalating number of child maltreatment reports. CPS workers have become extremely concerned about their ability to handle the ever increasing number of cases assigned to them for investigation. Workers' concerns are further magnified when they evaluate their effectiveness to render reports substantiated or unsubstantiated.

Along with escalating reporting comes an increase in the number of unfounded reports. Unfounded reports are largely a product of the emotionally charged desire for some individuals to "do something about child abuse" spurred on by media sensationalism (Besharov 1990). This is not to minimize the important role the media has played in alerting society to the problem of child maltreatment throughout the years. Nevertheless, its over zealous activities in reporting incidents of abuse and neglect has led to an understandable, but counterproductive overreaction by some professionals and citizens who report suspected child maltreatment (12). Now CPS agencies find themselves confronted with the results—growing numbers of unfounded reports.

The available data suggest that 65% of all reports after investigation are determined by CPS workers as unfounded (unsubstantiated) (12). This is a considerable increase from 1975 when only about 35 percent of all reports were unfounded (12). The high rate of unfounded reports contributes to the already overwhelming caseloads in CPS agencies, and further strains the already existing limited resources. Workers are increasingly unable to protect children in real danger because of staggering caseloads (12). With the increase in unfounded reports, workers' time is becoming less available to children who may indeed be at risk. CPS agencies also note that errors in judgement among workers are increasing as the system becomes more and more over-burdened. Furthermore, CPS workers report that unfounded cases begin to desensitize them to the obvious warning signals in a child's environment which denote immediate and serious danger. On a broader policy level the investigation of a large number of unfounded cases disrupts the fragile community consensus that supports state intervention on behalf of children.

Given the climate of society to encourage reporting of suspected child maltreatment, unfounded reporting is not surprising. Professionals suspecting abuse incidents, but who may not be certain, have been informed not to take the risk of not reporting. In many cases, these individuals are not sure of the signs and symptoms of abuse and do not know how to proceed in validating or ruling out their suspicions.

For example, Ms. Brown a child care worker in Agency Y Group Home noticed that seven-year-old Carol, a resident in the group home, had a large bruise on her right arm. When Ms. Brown asked Carol how she got the bruise, Carol said, "when I was with my mom this weekend." Ms. Brown made a report of abuse to the authorities. The report was rendered by CPS as unfounded because Ms. Brown did not fully obtain enough information about the circumstances of Carol's injury before she made the report. This example is not uncommon. Often when some mandated reporters are confronted with a child who has a physical injury they often do not know how and what information to seek about the possible occurrence of child maltreatment, nor do they recognize the verbal and non-verbal behaviors of maltreated children. In these situations, reporters are unable to make informed decisions before generating a report. They see the injury and with limited information make a report.

Situations like this suggest that many reporters are unclear about the role they must undertake in making a report to the authorities. Unfortunately many reporters, especially mandated reporters, perceive themselves as having to provide only minimal information when making a report. They do not understand that seeking necessary information regarding suspected incidents of abuse or neglect is critical to the well-being of the child and family. Many reporters do not understand they are often in a much better position than the CPS workers to obtain information. They see the investigating agency workers as having the total responsibility to collect the necessary information to determine the disposition for the case. These reporters are failing to understand their responsibilities in the reporting system.

Given the increase in reporting that has resulted in staggering caseloads of CPS workers and high rates of unfounded reports, there is a significant need to help the public and professionals better understand when a report should be made. To date the theory, research, and available educational materials are quite limited in providing reporters and investigators with an understanding of situations that warrant reporting children and their families.

AN OVERVIEW OF THE STUDY:
URBAN CHILD ABUSE REPORTING

Child abuse reporting in *urban* areas is a very familiar concern. Most practitioners, policy-makers, and administrators in urban child welfare agencies are increasingly recognizing the need to understand better what reporters see as constituting child abuse. Such information would enable child welfare agencies to work with reporters to help reduce the number of unfounded reports referred for investigation. Few studies have been put forth in the literature to examine urban child abuse reporting from this perspective.

This book will present a study conducted in *Baltimore, Maryland* on child abuse reporting. The study investigates urban child abuse reporting from the aspect of the kinds of reports made to the local CPS agency by reporters, and the types of case dispositions given to reports from different reporting sources. First, the study analyzes the differences in reports from medical and non-medical reporting sources in relationship to the characteristics of reported children and their families. The characteristics to be analyzed regarding reported children and their families include: 1) age, race, and sex of children; 2) type of abuse sustained by children; 3) severity of abuse; 4) alleged perpetrators of abuse; 5) ages of caretaker; and 6) socio-economic status of families. And secondly, it examines the differences in the rates of report substantiation according to whether the report came from a medical or non-medical reporting source.

The study presents findings that delineate the characteristics and dispositions of child abuse reports in relationship to the source of the reports. Such findings can help increase our theoretical and practical knowledge of child abuse reporting. With regard to theoretical development, the findings can serve as a basis to expand existing conceptual models, and to develop new frameworks that attempt to explain how various individuals and systems determine what is or is not abuse. For child welfare practice, the findings can facilitate them to gain a better understanding of the strengths and weaknesses of different reporters. In addition, child welfare practitioners can begin to utilize the information to develop new programs that address the gaps in knowledge some reporters have regarding child abuse. With greater knowledge of how reporting sources differ in what they report, practitioners and reporters can begin to work more collaboratively to help strengthen reporting of child abuse.

The subsequent chapters in this book will present the conceptual framework, research methodology, and findings of this study on urban child abuse reporting. Chapter 2 will review the available literature on child abuse reporting as it pertains to medical and non-medical reporters of abuse and case dispositions. Chapter 3 will discuss child abuse reporting from an ecological perspective. Chapter 4 presents the research methodology used in this study to examine reporting and investigatory results. Chapter 5 presents a description of the study sample. Chapter 6 provides the study findings. And, Chapter 7 offers discussion, and research and practice implications.

II

Reporting and Report Dispositions:
A Literature Review

The literature on child abuse reporting and report dispositions is quite scant. Over the years practitioners, researchers, and theoreticians have studied intensely the etiology of child maltreatment. The areas of child abuse reporting and case dispositions have not received the same attention. This review presents the literature on reporting sources, report characteristics, and report investigation. Specifically, it examines the reporting behaviors of medical and non-medical reporters of child abuse. Particular attention is directed toward the characteristics of: 1) age, race, and sex of children; 2) type of abuse sustained by children; 3) severity of abuse; 4) alleged perpetrators of abuse; 5) ages of caretakers; and 6) socio-economic status of families that medical and non-medical reporters make known in child abuse reports. Finally, the rate of report substantiation among reports from medical and non-medical reporting sources is discussed.

NATIONAL FINDINGS ON REPORTING, INVESTIGATIONS, AND DISPOSITIONS

Reporting Sources

National studies conducted in 1991 and 1993 indicate that more than half of all reports come from professional systems. As illustrated in Figure 2.1, schools (16.3 percent) are the largest reporting source of abuse and neglect, followed by legal organizations (12.4 percent) including law enforcement agencies and justice systems; social services agencies (11.7 percent);

medical organizations (10.7 percent) including emergency rooms and their staffs; and child care providers (1.6 percent), representing those reporting sources who are among the first to identify physical child abuse (U.S. Department of Health and Human Services 1995; Ginsberg 1995).

Figure 2.1

1993 Professional Reporting

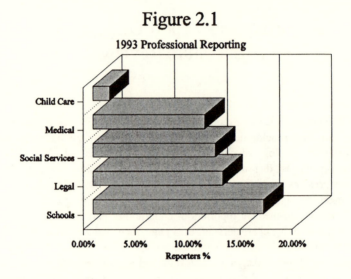

Source: U.S. Department of Health and Human Services, 1995

According to a 1993 study conducted by the U.S. Department of Health and Human Services (1995) family members of victims constituted 18 percent of the reporting sources. Of the family members identified as reporters, victims represent 1.4 percent, parents 6.6 percent, and other relatives 10.1 percent. Other reporting sources identified include anonymous reporters representing 11.0 percent; friends and neighbors 10.4 percent; others (no specific category given) 10.1 percent; and perpetrators 0.5 percent for the reports received (See Figure 2.2) (U.S. Department of Health and Human Services 1995). The percentages remained consistent for this period (2-2).

Figure 2.2

1993 Non-Professional Reporting

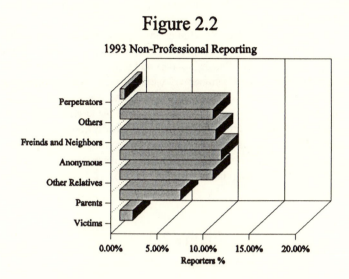

Source: U.S. Department of Health and Human Services, 1995

Demographics on Victims

Age of Victims: As children get older the percentage reported and substantiated for maltreatment decreases. In 1993, 51 percent of the victims were 7 years and younger, and approximately 26 percent were 3 years of age or younger. Children 13-18 years of age represented about one in five victims (2-8).

Sex of Victims: For the same study year, females were identified more often than males for child maltreatment. Females represented 51 percent of the victims, and males 45 percent. For about 4 percent of the victims, no information was available. When examining the finding on gender and type of maltreatment, females are twice as likely as males to be victims of sexual abuse.

Differences were also indicated for the type of maltreatment in relationship to the gender and age of victims. To illustrate, male victims younger than 12 are more likely than females the same age to be physically abused. But, for victims who are older than 12, females are more likely than males to be physically abused (2-9).

Ethnicity/Race of Victims: Six ethnic/racial groups were represented in the 1993 study: White Americans, African Americans, Hispanics, Native Americans, Asian American/Pacific Islanders and those of other ethnic/racial backgrounds. The largest number of victims were White Americans representing 54 percent, followed by African Americans constituting 25 percent, and 9 percent were Hispanics. Native Americans and other ethnic/racial background groups comprised individually about 2 percent of the victims. Asian American/Pacific Islanders represented only 0.8 percent, as depicted in Figure 2.3. The ethnicity/racial background was unknown for 8.5 percent of the victims in this study (2-10, 2-11).

Figure 2.3

1993 Ethnicity/Race of Victims

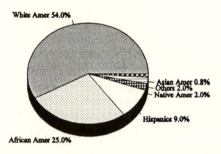

White Amer 54.0%

Asian Amer 0.8%
Others 2.0%
Native Amer 2.0%

Hispanics 9.0%

African Amer 25.0%

Source: U.S. Department of Health and Human Services, 1995

Child Fatalities: In regard to child fatalities, the findings reflect the deaths of children or siblings known to child protective services agencies as active and past clients at the time of death. Forty-six states reported a total of 1,028 children who died as a result of child maltreatment in 1993. In 1992, forty-three states reported 1,046 child fatalities. In 1993, there was a decrease in the number of fatalities, even with three more states reporting their child fatality statistics. Nevertheless, the child fatality rate for states reporting in 1993 was 1.62 per 100,000 the population under eighteen years of age. Accurate data on child fatalities is difficult to obtain (2-12). These findings may only represent the tip of the iceberg.

Perpetrators: Based on the 1993 findings of 40 reporting states, 9 out of every 10 perpetrators of child maltreatment investigated by a child protective services agency were either a parent or relative of the victim. Seventy-seven percent of the perpetrators were parents and 12 percent were relatives. Individuals in non-caretaking relationships to the child victims represented only 5 percent of the perpetrators. These percentages have remain quite stable over the last 4 years (2-12).

Report Investigations

Dispositions of Investigations: In 1993 an estimated 1.6 million investigations of alleged maltreatment were undertaken. About 38 percent of these investigations resulted in reported dispositions of either substantiated or indicated for maltreatment. Just over half of the reported dispositions for 1993, as in previous years, resulted in unsubstantiated or not indicated dispositions. Intentional false reports represented only about 6 percent of unsubstantiated dispositions. Reports closed without a finding or unknown dispositions represent only about 4 percent of all dispositions. Frequently, such dispositions included situations where families moved prior to the completion of the investigation (2-3). Only about 5 percent of the investigation dispositions were classified as "other." This category includes investigations where States could not use one of the existing dispositions categories (2-4).

Dispositions of Child Maltreatment Victims: In 1993, 1,018,692 children were determined to be victims of maltreatment. For this study year, dispositions of substantiated or indicated for maltreatment cases were rendered for 39 percent of the children and 45 percent of the children received dispositions of unsubstantiated or not indicated. Thirteen percent of the children received an investigation disposition of either no finding or unknown finding, and 3 percent of the children received a disposition of "other" (2-4).

To further examine the dispositions of victims, it is critical to recognize the state policies. State policies include two-tier dispositions (substantiated or unsubstantiated) and three-tier dispositions (substantiated, indicated or unsubstantiated). Approximately, 31 percent of children in two-tier states had an investigation that resulted in maltreatment being found, compared to 47 percent of children in three-tier states. In three-tier states, child victims were evenly divided between substantiated and indicated dispositions (2-5). These findings indicate distinct trends in reporting and investigations.

CHARACTERISTICS OF MEDICAL CHILD ABUSE REPORTING

Age, Race, and Sex of Children

Children reported most often by medical reporters were young (9 years and under), black, and male (Ginsberg 1995, 68; Hampton and Newberger 1985; Johnson and Shower 1985). Prior research also indicated that medical personnel (i.e., physicians, nurses, therapists, and social workers) more often reported young children between the ages of infancy and 9 years, minority children, and male children (Mayhill and Norgard 1983). Furthermore, as early as the 1940s, 50s and 60s landmark studies by Caffey (1946); Silverman (1953); Fontana (1964); Kempe (1962); and Holter and Friedman, (1968) showed that medical personnel indicated in records more younger children than older children as being victims of non-accidental injuries.

Some studies suggest that the attitudes of medical reporters may be biased toward reporting the young child. These studies suggest medical reporters report young children more often because they view young children as more vulnerable to sustaining injuries inflicted by an abusive caretaker. For older (adolescent) children unless injuries are severe, like internal trauma of such a serious degree that could not be explained, they are not

often seen as being abuse victims. Most of the medical personnel
interviewed in this study indicate that older children are viewed as more
likely to sustain many injuries accidentally through activities with peers than
younger children (Jason, et. al. 1982; Fontana 1973).

Research conducted with pediatricians indicated they reported minority
children more often than white children. The reporting behavior of the
pediatricians involved further indicated that reports alleging abuse of
minority children demonstrated greater details of the suspected abuse
incidents, while reports alleging abuse of white children were quite vague
(McPherson and Garica 1983). This research suggests a disparity in
reporting minority and white children for suspected child abuse. The
reporting disparity may be accounted for by the pediatricians' perceptions
about which racial group of children should be investigated most thoroughly
when abuse is suspected, and/or if at the time the pediatricians had more
information on the minority children to report. Whatever the reason, there is
an apparent need to understand why the disparity in reporting exists. It was
also found that inner-city physicians also reported a disproportionately
higher rate of minority children compared to white children, even when
white children represented a significant segment of the urban area
(McDonald and Reece 1979). The research suggest that the reporting
behavior of the physicians studied is skewed toward reporting minority
children more frequently then white children.

To further illustrate the reporting behaviors of physicians in relationship
to the age, race, and sex of alleged abused children, the following case
profiles are presented.

Case Profile 1: Mary a five-year-old white female was brought to
the emergency room of Hospital X complaining of stomach pains.
During the examination the physician found her abdomen to be
very tender, he ruled out appendicitis because Mary's appendix had
been removed. Some old bruises were present on her abdomen.
When Mary was asked about the stomach pain and bruises, she
said, "she fell." The doctor proceed to treat Mary and released her
to her mother and father. A week later Mary was readmitted to the
hospital with a ruptured spleen, fresh bruises, welts, and a bruised
kidney. Mary was being abused by her mother.
Case Profile 2: Robert a seven-year-old African American was
brought to Hospital X emergency room by his babysitter. She

indicated Robert had been complaining of pain in his arm for
several days. When the child was examined it was determined that
his arm had been fractured in two areas. The babysitter was unable
to provide any information about the circumstance of Robert's
injuries. A report was made to the authorities.

Type of Abuse

Much of the literature has been directed toward physical child abuse over the
years. But, with the expansion of child abuse reporting laws nationwide, to
include sexual abuse reporting, a few researchers have begun to examine the
trends in reporting of physical and sexual abuse among medical sources
(Besharov 1990; Reiniger, Robinson, McHugh 1995; Giovannoni and
Becerra 1979). Reporting patterns of practicing physicians indicate that they
report 91% of cases diagnosed as suspected physical abuse, and 92% of
cases diagnosed as suspected sexual abuse. The remaining 9% and 8%
respectively of cases not reported were due to physicians' reluctance to
report cases when they were not certain the diagnosis was abuse, and the
belief that they could work with the family to solve the problem without
outside intervention (Saulsbury and Campbell 1985).

It was also found that physicians more often report sexual abuse than
physical abuse. The difference in reporting was attributed to the attitudes of
the physicians regarding discipline and factors surrounding the alleged
incidents. Attitudes varied among physicians ranging from a child should not
be physically disciplined to physical discipline is acceptable within limits,
but the child should not be physically injured. The degree to which
physicians view physical discipline as appropriate influences their reporting
behavior surrounding physical abuse; because sexual abuse was not viewed
as appropriate physical discipline, physicians reported sexual abuse more
readily when they had evidence of such abuse. Other reasons stated by
physicians for not reporting physical abuse included the injury was not
serious, their familiarity with the family, parents demonstrated appropriate
concern, compatibility of history and physical examination, and the child
demonstrated no unusual behavior (Morris et al. 1985; Lassiter, 1987).

Child protective services' practitioners suggest that it is these kinds of
attitudes that can further endanger the lives of children and prevent families
from receiving needed intervention (Lindsey 1994; Besharov 1986; Mayhill

and Norgard 1983; Rosenfeld and Newberger 1977). Other CPS practitioners suggest that physicians should thoroughly examine situations before reporting (Besharov 1990; Besharov 1984). Practitioners do not agree, however, with physicians' decisions not to report cases that indicate abuse because they chose to work with the families themselves (Lindsey 1994; Reinhart 1983; Devlin 1983).

The following case profiles illustrate a snap shot of the types of abuse physicians may or may not report.

> **Case Profile 3**: Ellen, age 6, was taken by her grandmother to their family physician for her back-to-school physical examination. During the examination the physician found evidence that Ellen had been sexually molested. The physician spoke with the grandmother about the child's diagnosis. A report of alleged child sexual abuse was made by the physician.
>
> **Case Profile 4**: Mr. Brown a thirty-year-old engineer noticed multiple old and new scratches and welts on his eight-year-old daughter's arms. When asking the child's mother about the injuries, she said, "Valerie is just an accident prone child. She will grow out of it." Mr. Brown took Valerie to the pediatrician who assured him that the injuries were only minor. Mr. Brown informed the pediatrician of what his wife had said. The pediatrician responded by saying, "I will speak with Mrs Brown about how to better handle Valerie." Mr. Brown left the office feeling the physician knew best. No report was made by the physician about suspected abuse.

Severity of Abuse

Since Kempe (1962) and his associates introduced the terminology of "the battered child syndrome" much attention has been directed toward documenting child abuse based on the injuries sustained by a child. Even before Kempe's landmark work, Caffey (1946) and Silverman (1953) used x-rays to detect non-accidental physical injuries to children. Severity of injury is a critical factor in child abuse reporting for medical reporters given the nature of the settings in which they encounter suspected incidents of abuse.

Medical personnel define inflicted trauma as a critical factor in deciding to report suspected child abuse incidents (Besharov 1990; Holter and Friedman 1968; and Fontana 1973). They report most often children with multiple bruises and welts (135; 781). Medical personnel also significantly report children with internal trauma, multiple fracture, second and third degree burns, subdural hematomas, and evidence of sexual molestation and venereal disease (Fontana and Besharov 1977; Newberger and Bourne 1978; Besharov 1990).

It is not surprising that the literature over the years suggest medical personnel focus their attention toward the degree to which a child sustained non-accidental physical injuries and/or was sexually abused. While such evidence of abuse is critical, it is also important that medical reporters recognize other factors that indicate abuse in the absence of severe injury to the child, (i.e., changes in child's behavior when questioned about injury, inconsistencies in how injury happened, attitude of parents, etc.).

Presented, as follows, are examples of cases that denote incidents pertaining to severity of abuse that get reported by medical personnel.

Case Profile 5: William, age 4, was bought to the hospital unconscious. His stepfather and mother stated William fell from a tree in their backyard. From the x-rays taken, the technician and physician discovered that William had multiple old fractures, previous internal trauma, and a subdural hematoma. When asked about William's medical history, the parents said, "William has only been seen by doctors for colds." The parents also held to the story about William's fall from the tree. A report of alleged physical abuse was made to the authorities by the physician.

Case Profile 6: Marsha, age 18 months, and her mother were in a car accident. The paramedics examined both mother and Marsha. The paramedics found multiple burns on the child's buttocks, and cuts and bruises on several other areas of the child's body. All of the injuries were recent. The paramedics were sure these injuries were not related to the car accident, because the child was in a safety seat. The paramedics suggested that the mother and child have a follow-up appointment at the hospital. The mother refused when she observed the paramedics examining the child's body. The paramedics made an immediate report to the local child protective services agency.

Age of Caretakers

The literature on the risk of abuse to children in relationship to the age of the caretakers (i.e., parents, or guardians) responsible for the care of the child is quite limited. However, the few studies looking at age of caretakers indicate medical reporters more often report young mothers, under 25 years of age, for abuse than older mothers, because they see young mothers as being more likely to use physical measures when disciplining (Howing et al. 1993; Hampton and Newberger 1985; Johnson and Shower 1985; Taylor and Newberger 1979; Giovannoni and Becerra 1979; England and Brunnquell 1979). Further research indicates that families with both parents under the age of 25 were reported more frequently by medical systems than families where one or both parents were over age 25 (Mayhill and Norgard 1983). In contrast, other studies found that older parents were most often alleged in reports of severe physical abuse and sexual molestation (Sheldon et al. 1985; Oates 1984; Rabb 1981). But, from these studies older parents were still reported less than younger parents overall.

Alleged Perpetrators

In recent years increased attention has been directed toward examining who are the perpetrators of abuse. Mothers have traditionally been labeled the primary perpetrators of child maltreatment. But, as the problem of sexual abuse becomes more visible and physical abuse continues to increase, both male and female caretakers are found to be perpetrators of abuse.

Physicians and other medical personnel report mothers most often as perpetrators of child physical abuse, both in single parent and two parent homes (Ditson and Shay 1984). Medical personnel also reported natural fathers more often as perpetrators in sexual abuse against female children. Further findings showed that medical personnel report older non-relative males known to the female child for sexual abuse (Geiser 1979; Faller, Froning, and Lipovsky 1991). In medical reports, boys experienced sexual abuse through homosexual encounters with older men known to them. Most often step-fathers were alleged as the perpetrators of these acts (Pierce and Pierce 1985).

From these studies on medical reporting, it appears that the gender and relationship of the perpetrator(s) to the child is related to the type of abuse perpetrated. Such findings suggest that children are vulnerable to certain types of abuse from different individuals with whom they are familiar.

Families Socio-Economic Status (SES)

The role socio-economic status plays as a determinant of child abuse has become a controversial issue. Several studies indicate medical reporters report lower socio-economic status families at a greater rate for abuse than middle and upper class families (Giovannoni and Becerra 1979; Garbarino 1980; Hampton 1987a).

Further research examining the reporting behaviors of pediatricians supports this trend. Pediatricians tended to over-represent the poor in abuse reports and under-represent middle and upper class families regardless of where they were in practice (urban or suburban settings). It was found that pediatricians often labeled suspected child abuse in affluent families as accidents and did not report those families (McPherson and Garcia 1983).

Other studies showed physicians who had practices in both inner-city and suburban areas demonstrate skewed reporting behaviors. Physicians reported middle and upper income families in their suburban practices at a very low rate. While, in their inner-city practices low income families were reported at a substantially high rate. Such disparities in reporting between suburban and inner-city areas seems suspicious and may suggest reporting bias. It is postulated that a low rate of reporting in suburban areas may be related to medical reporters' over-identification with such families who represent their same or similar socio-economic status. And, the high rate of reporting low income families in inner-city areas may be influenced by stereotypes reporters have about abusive families (McDonald and Reece 1979; Lindsey 1994). Essentially, these studies suggest that the reporting patterns of medical reporters are skewed toward reporting low-income families.

The following case profiles illustrate the age of caretakers, alleged perpetrators, and reported families socio-economic status that medical reporters most often report.

Case Profile 7: Thomas, age 5, was reported to the local authorities by a staff nurse from an inner-city HMO for alleged child abuse. Thomas was initially brought into the HMO for treatment of a dog bite. The child had fresh bruises on his face, and multiple marks and cuts on his buttocks and back that resembled a strap or belt. His mother is age 22 and father is age 23. The family reside in a low income community in the inner-city. When speaking with Thomas' parents about the bruises, cuts, and marks, his mother stated he is a hyper-child who must be constantly corrected. From the child protective services investigation, the report was substantiated for abuse and the mother was the perpetrator of the abuse.

Case Profile 8: Nancy, age 12, was visiting with her grandparents. Nancy was taken to the hospital clinic with complaints of severe cramps. The physician found the child had sustained vaginal trauma. When Nancy was asked by the social worker about her sexual activities, she became withdrawn, and fearful. She denied having sex with boys or being raped by any boy. Nancy stated "she just wanted to live with her grandparents and did not want to return home." She was extremely afraid to discuss her injury. Her grandparents were astounded. A report of sexual abuse was made by the hospital social worker. Upon investigation it was found that Nancy's natural father had been sexually abusing her since she was about age 5.

Case Profile 9: Allen, age 9, lives in an extended family household with his father's relatives. Allen's mother took him to the pediatrician because she had noticed a consistent discharge in his soiled underwear. The pediatrician examined the child and found evidence of sexual molestation. A report of child sexual abuse was made to the authorities. It was found that Allen's uncle, his father's 42-year-old brother, was the perpetrator.

Overall, the literature on the characteristics of children, their families, and perpetrators reported by medical reporters suggest that these reporters do not report a cross-section of the population. It suggests that medical reporters primarily report young children, minority children, male children, and those who reside in poverty areas. A combination of factors seem to influence their reporting. One factor may be bias. A second possible factor may be that they encounter a limited population of maltreated children.

CHARACTERISTICS OF NON-MEDICAL
CHILD ABUSE REPORTING

Even though the number of studies of medical child abuse reporting is low, studies examining the reporting behavior of non-medical reporters are fewer still. This section of the review discusses the available literature on child abuse reporting among non-medical reporters.

Age, Race, and Sex of Children

Caseworkers in public and private agencies reported adolescents for abuse more often then other reporters. It was found adolescents are more often not reported for abuse because they are able to escape the abuser and avoid serious injury(ies). Because young children cannot often escape their abuser, they are more vulnerable to sustaining injuries that lead to them being reported. When examining reports of physical abuse, caseworkers reported young children and adolescents equally when this type of maltreatment was present. Other studies indicated some caseworkers in public and private social agencies reported children younger than nine years more often. Further examination into the reporting behaviors of caseworkers indicate that the largest proportion of children reported for physical injuries and/or sexual acts perpetrated against them are three years old and younger. Female children were reported more often by caseworkers for sexual abuse (Lindsey 1994; Farber and Joseph 1985; DiLeonardi 1980).

Black children have been over-represented in reports of child abuse since the inception of the collection of national data (Hampton, Gelles, and Harrop 1991). Non-medical reporters have not been immune from this reporting trend. Even in 1980 when black children comprised only 14% of all the children in the population, they represented 21% of the reported child abuse cases from both non-medical and medical reporting sources (Lauderdale 1980). Survey data on child abuse over the years have not deviated from black children being reported at a higher rate than their white counterparts (Hampton, Gelles, and Harrop 1991).

From the literature pertaining to the race of reported children, black children were the dominant group. This could mean that black children are abused more often, or that reporters have a bias to report these children. The characteristic of age demonstrated that these reporters report both young children and adolescents. The available research suggest females were more often reported for sexual abuse by non-medical reporters.

Severity of Abuse

Because of the legal definition of abuse (or injury) the central fact in a report is to provide legal evidence of injury. Consequently, non-medical reporters like medical sources report cases according to severity of injury. School personnel make reports based on the following factors: 1) skin infection, lesions, and bruises; 2) neurological manifestation—i.e., coordination problems; 3) gastro-intestinal manifestations—i.e., abdominal pain, and spontaneous vomiting; 4) injuries that are explained with weak explanations; 5) changes in child's moods or overt physical actions toward other children and adults, or toward inanimate objects; and 6) incidents reported by victims. School personnel are in the best position to observe these criteria because of their daily contact with children. Severity of injury causes teachers and other school personnel to report child abuse (Howing et al. 1993; Turbett and O'Toole 1983; McCaffrey and Tewey 1978; ten Bensel and Berdie 1976; Manley-Casimir and Newman 1976).

Police most often report incidents of obvious injury to children (Giovannoni and Becerra 1979; Nagi 1977; Schmitt 1978). Approximately, 70% of the reports from police officers denote severe sexual and/or physical injury (Giovannoni and Becerra 1979). A popular theory police suggest is that their reporting behavior is a result of their training. Police are trained and given the role to respond to acts of violence that are perpetrated in society (Flammang 1981). Therefore, they are highly sensitive to the most violent acts perpetrated and may devalue lesser actions.

With regard to severity of abuse, caseworkers in public and private social agencies were also found to report incidents of physical injury including burns, scars, welts, and bruises more often. Caseworkers are reluctant to report incidents when concrete evidence of injury is not available and the child could not provide accurate information (DiLeonardi 1980).

Anonymous callers most often reported physical abuse of children that included cuts, bruises, and welts. The next most often reported physical abuse were burns, fractures, subdural hematomas and internal injuries (Adams et al. 1982). In a study comparing anonymous reporting in Baltimore City, Maryland, and Bronx County, New York; Baltimore City anonymous callers reported more incidents of severe injuries (Zuravin et al. 1987a,b). These studies suggest that anonymous callers observe and report serious incidents of abuse.

To illustrate, the following case profiles present reports made by non-medical reporters.

Case Profile 10: Jason, an African American age 13, resides in a boys' group home. He was referred to the case manager for aggressively acting out in his cottage. This was unusual behavior for Jason. The case manager asked Jason about his relationship with the other boys and staff in his cottage. Jason said, "he was fine with the other boys." He did not mention the staff at all. When further questioned about the staff he refused to answer. The case manager became suspicious of Jason's non-verbal behavior regarding the staff. The case manager talked with other boys in the cottage and different staff. The case manager made a report of suspected abuse to the agency administrator alleging a staff person as the perpetrator. The agency administrator made the report to the authorities.

Case Profile 11: Laura, age 3, and Bryan, age 2, were reported by an anonymous reporter to the local child protective services agency. The reporter indicated seeing numerous bruises, cuts, lesions, and welts on the children's legs. The reporter also indicated that Bryan had a scalding like mark on his back. The reporter wished to remain anonymous.

From the available literature pertaining to non-medical reporters, it appears the characteristics reported differ somewhat among the reporters in these groups. These reporters tended more often to report children, who sustained less visible injuries. The literature delineating the reporting behavior of non-medical reporters is quite limited. There is also a significant void in the literature regarding the characteristics that neighbors, friends, parents, the victims and other lay individuals make known in reports of suspected child abuse.

The final section of this review discusses the rate of report substantiation and unsubstantiation between medical and non-medical sources.

RATE OF REPORT SUBSTANTIATION AND UNSUBSTANTIATION

Studies over the years have shown that approximately six out of every ten reports of child abuse are not substantiated for abuse (U.S. Department of Health and Human Services 1995; Besharov 1990, 1986; Burnley 1986). This high rate of unsubstantiation has researchers and practitioners concerned, because as child abuse reporting continues to increase the system is steadily inundated with unfounded reports. Therefore, it is imperative that practitioners understand better when reporters are erroneously reporting or when further follow-up is needed with the reporters to obtain further documentation of abuse. These practical activities can best be undertaken when practitioners have further knowledge of reporting behavior to enhance their ability to substantiate or not substantiate a report for abuse.

Earlier studies indicate that law enforcement agency reports were substantiated more often then reports from medical sources (Groenveld and Giovannoni 1977; Giovannoni 1980). The substantiation rate among physical abuse reports from law enforcement agencies was 94% (Giovannoni 1980). These studies suggest that the high rate of report substantiation for law enforcement agencies is due to their high rate of reporting incidents of obvious severe injury to the child. Overall, reports from medical reporters (i.e., hospitals, clinics and private physicians) were substantiated more often than reports from non-medical reporters such as schools, public/private social agencies and lay persons (Groenveld and Giovannoni 1977).

Other research revealed that the rate of report substantiation for physical abuse allegations was increasing for reports from school. The substantiation rate for sexual abuse allegations are increasing also for school systems (Abramczyk and Sweigart 1985).

Reports from anonymous sources are less likely to be substantiated than reports from medical reporting sources. Further findings indicate non-medical reporters such as neighbors, friends, parents, relatives, the victims and other lay individuals are twice as likely to be substantiated by the investigative caseworker, than reports from anonymous reporters (Zuravin et. al. 1987a,b).

From the available studies, the substantiation rate for law enforcement reporting is becoming comparable to that of medical reports. This is largely due to the consistency with which law enforcement officials respond to the most violent situations of abuse. The literature does suggest that when comparing medical reports to non-medical reporters (schools, public/private social agencies, and lay persons), omitting law enforcement agencies, medical reports were substantiated more often. Further research into the area of report substantiation is needed for practitioners to effectively handle issues surrounding the high rate of report unsubstantiation.

From the literature, it is clear that there is limited empirical evidence as to what the differences are between medical and non-medical reporters in terms of abuse allegations, severity of abuse, and the types of children, families, and perpetrators reported. It is also evident that for medical reporters other factors in our society play a key role in what gets reported. Such societal factors influencing reporting include reporter's training, personal beliefs about what constitutes child maltreatment, how maltreatment should be handled, and the types of environments in which they encounter suspected incidents (i.e., hospital, school, social agency, or neighborhood). Child abuse reporting involves a diverse network of members in the community who represent many social settings and views on child abuse. In Chapter 3 child abuse reporting is discussed from an ecological perspective in order to better understand what factors may indeed influence reporters to report or not report suspected incidents of maltreatment.

III

An Ecological Perspective on Child Abuse Reporting

Many theoretical perspectives have been put forth to explain the problem of child maltreatment (abuse). Theoretical explanations have come from the psychological, sociological and social psychological schools of thought. In recent years theoreticians, researchers and practitioners, alike, have begun to view child maltreatment from an ecological perspective. The ecological perspective integrates social and psychological insights. According to the ecological perspective child maltreatment (abuse) involves forces at work in the individual, in the family, and in the community and culture in which the individual and the family are embedded (Crittenden 1992; Belsky 1980; Gelles 1980; Alvy 1975; Park and Collmer 1975; Starr, Beresnie, and Rossi 1976). Maltreatment is the result of the interaction of forces in the individual, his/her family, social networks, and community. These explanations have been used over the years to address the etiology of child abuse. The ecological perspective provides a comprehensive framework for analyzing the many different aspects of child maltreatment. It presents a theoretical foundation for examining the socio-economic factors (i.e., economic status), demographic factors (i.e., values and attitudes within communities and cultures), and the developmental factors that represent the characteristics of communities and individual relationships; all factors that impact on the reporting and investigation of child abuse (Krishman and Morrison 1995).

Child abuse reporting as differentiated from child abuse has received limited attention in the literature. Studies conducted years ago by Taylor and Newberger (1979); Blumberg (1974); Paulson (1974); and Billingsley and Giovannoni (1972) suggest that numerous factors in our society impact significantly on what individuals report and substantiate as abuse. Such

31

findings indicated that child abuse reporting, like other aspects of the child maltreatment problem, is also influenced by factors embedded in our society (Lauderdale 1980). To analyze the phenomenon of child abuse reporting, the author has adopted insights of the ecological perspective.

ECOLOGICAL ANALYSIS OF REPORTING

The phenomenon of child abuse reporting can be analyzed using the ecological perspective by calling attention to the systems involved. According to Bronfenbrenner (1979) there are four types of systems that influence individuals and their functioning in society. These systems include the microsystems, mesosystems, exosystems, and macrosystems. Microsystems are systems that include individuals with whom a person has direct contact, such as family members, friends, co-workers, and professionals. Mesosystems are systems in which a person may not be a member but which directly affect the person's behavior, especially their decision making. Exosystems are bureaucratic structures (systems) that impact on groups without having knowledge of any specific individual affected, i.e., legislative bodies that make funding decisions, administrators who decide what services to offer, and courts that set precedents. Finally, macrosystems represent cultural and subcultural influences that affect individuals and institutions through values, traditions and role expectation.

In the child abuse reporting arena each of these systems impact on the decision making process of reporters. Reporters represent many different formal and informal systems in society. Therefore, how they view child abuse encompasses the norms of the formal and informal system(s) in which they are embedded as well as their own personal cultural and subcultural beliefs and values about abuse.

Reporters of abuse frequently operate within microsystems. The reporters work environment is an important microsystem in the child abuse reporting arena. For the most part, in the workplace reporters have direct contact with the children and the families which they decide to report for suspected abuse. Work environments influence the reporting behavior of the reporters in those settings. For example, physicians and other medical personnel more often report children who have serious physical injury and fewer children with minimal to no signs or symptoms of physical injuries.

This reporting behavior can be somewhat attributed to the population of children and families serviced in the systems (hospital emergency rooms, clinics, private offices) where they work. For physicians and other medical personnel, their understanding and exposure to the different signs and symptoms of abused children in the absence of visible physical injury may be limited. Therefore, if they are not familiar with the other indicators that may denote abuse, beyond just physical injury, a report may not be made.

Reporter's decision to report also represents the influences of mesosystems. Mesosystems represent persons, such as boards of directors, agency executives, and supervisors, who have the ability to directly affect the reporter's behavior without actually having contact with the children and/or families the reporter encounters. To illustrate, an agency board of directors establishes a policy within the agency for handling child abuse reporting. While such a policy may be of benefit, it can influence how reporters view their role and decisions about making known incidents of child abuse they suspect with clients. Essentially, the reporting behavior of reporters is often immediately affected in situations of this nature, because of the internal positions mesosytems may hold within an organizations .

Reporters have an interconnected relationship with exosystems. For example, reporters provide child welfare investigatory agencies with reports of suspected abuse. Reporters influence what agencies investigate as suspected incidents of abuse. To further illustrate, child welfare investigatory agencies are being confronted with a large number of unfounded cases. Investigatory agency have very little recourse but to investigate the reports they receive from reporters, especially professionals responsible for the care of children. Exosystems also influence reporters. These systems affect the behavior of reporters through legislated laws that require mandated reporting and significant penalties if they do not. To paraphrase, exosystems and reporters mutually influence each other.

Reporters are participatory members of macrosystems. In their role as reporters of suspected incidents of abuse, they influence the well-being of at risk families and their children, facilitate child protective services agencies to identify children and families in need of services, and furthermore through their reporting they help to maintain the cultural values and role expectations put forth in society to protect our children from harm.

First in using the ecological perspective, it allow us to understand that reporting sources are constantly adjusting to both internal and external influences. Second, reporters are interactive systems; meaning they are not only influenced but they do a great deal of influencing. Third, reporters in the child abuse reporting arena are extremely interconnected. This interconnectedness is vertical (micro to macro) and horizontal (member of one microsystem may have membership in another microsystem). Child abuse reporting is often misconstrued as an isolated behavior on the part of reporters. Reporting is, however, a very complex and dynamic process for the reporter that he or she may not fully recognize (Crittenden 1992).

Essentially, child abuse reporting is a network of systems involved in an ongoing decision making process about the occurrence of abuse. The unique characteristic of the child abuse reporting arena is that it involves both formal and informal systems in the network. When examining child abuse reporting from an ecological perspective it enables us to look at the act of reporting as intensely as the act of maltreatment. Therefore, the ecological perspective introduces a conceptual framework for analyzing what reporters make known as abuse and what investigatory agencies are able to substantiate.

The decisions reporters make regarding suspected incidents of abuse are influenced by the social situations in which they encounter the incidents and the cultural stereotypes about who are maltreaters and the children that are maltreated (Garbarino 1977, 1979). The social situations where reporters encounter incidents of abuse represent a variety of formal and informal social systems, i.e., work place, neighborhood, family setting, and informal social network (Bronfenbrenner 1977; Garbarino 1979; Mayhill and Norgard 1983). Each of these social systems represent a multitude of self-defined or legally mandated procedures, levels of expertise, and resources for handling child maltreatment.

Factors Influencing Reporting in Formal and Informal Social Systems

Self defined or legally mandated procedures in formal social systems can promote or constrain reporter's decisions about what and who to report. To illustrate, many agency guidelines direct some staff to make known their suspicions of abuse to designated individuals in the agency, (i.e., social workers, school principals, psychologists, therapists, agency administrators, etc.), before a report can be made to the authorities. In some situations, non-mandated reporters feel that these procedures help lend creditability to incidents they suspect are abuse. On the other hand, some staff are discouraged from reporting, because they feel like second class citizens in the reporting of abuse, or they wish not to deal with the agency process for making known their suspicions. Therefore, the decision to report and what is reported are often affected by procedures many formal social systems perceive as helpful.

In formal social systems the level of expertise to identify suspected incidents of abuse varies. Most often reporters of abuse are trained in disciplines (i.e., teaching, medicine, law enforcement, etc.) that do not provide them with a thorough understanding of the many facets of child maltreatment. There is no doubt that numerous formal systems have highly trained professionals who are responsible for the care of children. Nevertheless, their knowledge of child abuse is still often quite limited. For example, classroom teachers are in daily direct contact with children which allows them a greater opportunity to identify maltreatment. But, their training is primarily in teaching children to learn, not how to assess maltreatment. While, their course of study includes childhood development, it is not designed to encompass the multitude of behaviors that abused children may exhibit. The same is the case with physicians who may encounter numerous children. Physicians are trained to treat disease. In many cases a child may go unreported by a physician, because there is no physical injury that would denote abuse and their knowledge of other indicators (behavioral) are often limited.

Often formal social systems may not possess the resources to handle child maltreatment. Frequently staff in child care agencies who are potential reporters of abuse may be overwhelmed with the daily activities of the job, often due to temporary employee shortages, and innocently overlooking situations that may not obviously indicate child abuse. Even, child protective services (CPS) agencies are experiencing the effects of limited resources to handle child maltreatment. CPS agencies are confronted with growing numbers of reported cases they must investigate. These agencies often lack the most valuable resource (staff) to effectively handle the task confronting them. In the case of resource availability, it has a systemic impact on both the reporting and investigative processes of child abuse.

Furthermore, formal social systems influence child abuse reporting by the population of children and families they serve. For example, reporters (day care workers, teachers, adolescent counselors, etc) are often limited to a specific population of children, i.e., infants, toddlers, school age children, and adolescents. This limitation within formal systems is most important to understand. Individuals in these setting have the ability to familiarize themselves with the children and their families. It also affords them the opportunity to recognize what represents developmental issues for a child and situations that may indicate maltreatment.

Individuals reporting child abuse from informal systems (i.e., neighborhoods, family settings, etc.) are also confronted with many issues that influence their decisions to report abuse. For example, a parent who reports another parent for the abuse of their child is often confronted with the anger and threats of the other parent for making the report. In addition, the reporting parent feels guilty for making the report. This disrupts the family in most cases to the point of separation, divorce, or violence perpetrated against the reporting parent. The abusive parent often feels betrayed. In another situation, a parent may decide to remain silent regarding the abuse because they feel they can protect the child(ren) even when they are being abused themselves. For reporters who are family members, their decisions to report represents a high level of personal investment.

Neighbors are a part of the informal system of reporters. The decisions of neighbors to report in good faith is related to the repercussions they feel will occur as a result of them making the report. Even though, many states permit anonymous reporting, numerous individuals are still hesitate to make reports. Frequently, the information reported by neighbors and other members of informal social systems about suspected abuse is extremely scant.

Nevertheless, informal reporters represent a major role in the child abuse reporting arena. These individuals are indigenous reporters who reside in the neighborhoods and communities where most of the abuse of children occur. Therefore, their proximity to at risk families (i.e., impoverished conditions, unsafe housing, substance abuse, domestic violence, etc.) affords them the opportunity to alert authorities to the problems that are occurring in the household, even when abuse can not be substantiated.

Overall, these aspects of the social system where reporters encounter abuse can enhance or constrain their decisions to report suspected abuse incidents. Thus, the ecological perspectives provides a foundation for understanding the influences formal and informal social systems have on reporter's decisions to make known suspected incidents of child abuse.

The Impact of Cultural Stereotypes on Reporting

Mayhill and Norgard (1983) acknowledge that cultural stereotyping can foster the identification or non-identification and reporting of abuse. These authors suggest that quite often people maintain a variety of stereotypes regarding abused children, reported families, and individuals who are most likely to perpetrate abuse. Stereotypes can skew reporting toward or away from certain populations.

Cultural stereotypes greatly influence the types of children and families who are reported for abuse. It is well documented that low income and minority children and their families are most frequently reported for abuse. This reporting behavior is often attributed to the stereotypes that exist about low income and minority families. These stereotypes influence bias in reporting.

Several stereotypes regarding child rearing practices of certain groups in our society bias child abuse reporting. These stereotypes about child rearing practices are often associated with the factors of race and socio-economic status. Although some forms of child disciplining is usually viewed as necessary in responsible parenting, stereotypes that suggest abusive disciplining practice is pervasive among certain ethnic and socio-economic groups have negated the belief that there can be appropriate disciplining practices among these groups. Unfortunately, some reporters of abuse embrace these stereotypes. For example, there is the stereotype that African Americans as a group are considered more violent than white Americans (Hampton 1987). There are some reporters who have incorporated this stereotype in their thinking regarding African American behavior. Frequently, they become over zealous in their reporting of African American children for suspected incidents of abuse. This over reaction, on their part, is largely due to this stereotype about African Americans, not necessarily the situations they encounter with the children and families. This stereotype influences reporters to think that by virtue of race an act of violence was perpetrated.

Another stereotype regarding child rearing practices that influences some reporter's decisions about who are maltreaters and what children are being maltreated pertains to low income families. This stereotype suggest that families who live in poverty use abusive disciplinary practices when dealing with their children, more so then other socio-economic groups. This stereotype is a result of the faulty belief that families in poverty lack the knowledge to properly discipline their children and they abuse as a result of the stresses of poverty.

Some individuals who encounter situations of excessive parental discipline ascribe to the belief that parents with whom they are familiar, and are members of their same socio-economic or racial group can be helped by them and should not be referred to the authorities. This belief is most endangering to the well-being of the child(ren) in these at-risk families. This type of thinking, indeed, suggest that there is a bias among some reporters about how different groups of people should be handled regarding child abuse, public-vs-private intervention.

Several stereotypes about single female-headed-households exist that influence reporting. These households have been the target of stereotypes that suggest that children residing in these families are at risk of abuse because of the parental stress a single mother is confronted with in caring for her child(ren) alone. The underlying premise of this stereotype is that these mothers project their frustration onto their children abusively. This stereotype suggests like those previously mentioned that there is much misunderstanding about groups in society who differ from the majority group.

As stereotypes influence reporting it is important for us to recognize that there is a tremendous lack of understanding about cultural and subcultural differences in our society. It is critical that we begin to address this gap in knowledge, awareness, and sensitivity about differences in cultures, especially for child abuse reporters. We must also recognize how deep rooted stereotypes maybe. Many individuals in society rely on their personal beliefs and their social networks when making decisions. And, in some instances, reporters are no different in their decision making process. Therefore, it is critical that individuals and systems who are reporters of abuse become aware of the negative impact stereotypes have on children and their families. These stereotypes over scrutinize some children and their families, and place others at further risk. For those reporters who ascribe to stereotypes, their objectivity about certain children and families is undoubtedly skewed. It is unfortunate that most stereotypes affect individuals who are members of either a racial or economic minority group. This places these groups in a most vulnerable position to be excessively reported. The subsequent sections discusses the decision making process of medical and non-medical reporters of child abuse.

THE DECISION MAKING PROCESS FOR MEDICAL AND NON-MEDICAL CHILD ABUSE REPORTERS

The social system of reporters (i.e., work settings, neighborhoods, families, social networks, etc.), and the beliefs they maintain about child maltreatment influences significantly the criteria used, type of evidence provided, and judgments made regarding suspected incidents of child abuse (Nagi, 1977). These factors are discussed in this ecological perspective on child abuse reporting from the perspective of reporters in medical and non-medical systems. Medical and non-medical reporters represent a cross-section of informal and formal community systems. They also provide a multitude of perceptions regarding what individuals acknowledge as child abuse.

Medical Reporters

Reporters in health care settings (medical reporters) use physical and sexual injury to children as the primary criteria for determining abuse. They also evaluate the injury sustained in relationship to age and sex of the child. Based on such criteria medical reporters, because of the nature of the setting and their training, are able to provide concrete evidence that supports the decision that injury(ies) (i.e., fractures, internal trauma, bruises, welts, bites, molestation, and death) to the child were non-accidental.

The decisions that medical personnel, (and all others), make regarding whether to report or not report suspected incidents of abuse is influenced by their training, experiences with the problem, and their personal beliefs regarding the types of children and families at risk of child maltreatment (abuse) (McPherson and Garcia 1983; Mayhill and Norgard 1983; Garbarino 1979). Physicians' training in medical problems will direct them to medically significant evidence rather than behavioral characteristics (Mayhill and Norgard 1983).

Furthermore, studies by Jason et al. (1982) and Fontana (1973) indicated that reporting of suspected child abuse incidents by medical reporters is often biased by the setting and personal views. These authors suggest that medical reporters are more likely to report more severe incidents of physical and sexual injuries because medical settings are the primary system for the treatment of illnesses/injuries. Additionally, the high reporting rates of young children, minority children, and low-income families have been addressed by Jason et al. (1982) and Fontana (1973) from the perspective of the geographic location of the facilities, and the reporters' stereotypical views of child maltreatment. The location of the facility can bias the types of children and families that medical reporters make known, especially when the population served is over-represented by a particular racial or economic group. However, Mayhill and Norgard (1983) found that in settings where the population was mixed on these factors, there still remained a higher reporting rate of young children, minority children, and lower socio-economic families. Mayhill and Norgard (1983) suggest that personal bias of reporters is evident. Medical reporters (physicians) reported minority and low-income children more often for abuse because they saw these families as using physical discipline more often than non-minority middle to upper income families (Mayhill and Norgard 1983; Morris et al. 1985). Of course it is also possible that minority and low income families do abuse more than non-minority and non-low income families. For the purposes of this study the insights of Mayhill and Norgard (1983) and Morris et al. (1985) that stereotyping can lead to over-reporting of minority and low income children and under-reporting of white middle and upper class children is an important contribution.

Non-Medical Reporters

School personnel (non-medical reporters) use criteria for identifying incidents of suspected abuse which includes not only external appearance of injury, but the child's behavior. Specifically, the indicators of abuse used by school personnel include: 1) changes in the child's mood or overt physical actions toward other children and adults; 2) external injuries—i.e., bruises, welts, scars, and burns; and 3) incidents reported by victims. School personnel document in reports the physical injuries and behavioral changes in children they observe. These reporters are limited, however, in their abilities to provide concrete evidence (i.e., x-rays, or medical reports) to support their allegations. They are also unable in many cases to provide evidence of abuse in the absence of physical injury, even when they strongly suspect the child was or is being abused (Turbett and O'Toole 1983).

These reporters have a distinct advantage, however, that other reporters do not have. They are able to provide evidence of abuse situations that manifest over time (ten Bensel and Berdie 1976; McCaffrey and Tewey 1978; Manley-Casimir and Newman 1976). School reporters see children on a daily basis which allows them greater access to monitor and document incidents they identify as suspicious. Thus, in many instance situations that school personnel may report often go unreported by other reporters in settings where access to the child is limited to one or two encounters (Mayhill and Norgard 1983).

The decisions of school reporters to report or not report suspected incidents of child abuse, like medical reporters, involves their training, experience with the problem, and their personal beliefs regarding the types of children and families at risk of child maltreatment (Garbarino 1979). These reporters are trained for the most part in techniques of education. Most school reporters (i.e., teachers, and administrators) possess limited background in assessing the social dynamics of dysfunctional family systems. Some of the behavior that an abused child may exhibit may be unfamiliar to school personnel who have limited knowledge on which to evaluate such behavior as indicators of abuse (Turbett and O'Toole 1983).

School personnel in comparison to other non-medical reporters and medical reporters do more often encounter a more diverse population of children in terms of age, sex, and socio-economic status of family. However, in some school settings reporters may be at the same disadvantages as medical reporters. For example, an elementary school with a student enrollment of children aged 5 to 10 years would limit reporters to reporting on younger children. And, the same would exist for school reporters in settings where the racial and sex composition of students, socio-economic status of children's families, geographic location, and governance board (public or private) is skewed toward one particular group.

In addition, Richey (1980) suggests that school reporters who do not report suspected child abuse often do not want to get involved for fear of interfering in parents' rights to discipline their children. Such views suggest that these school reporters have strong personal values and beliefs regarding parental rights and child-rearing practices that can undoubtedly place a number of children and their families at risk of child maltreatment.

Neighbors, friends, relatives/parents, victims, and anonymous callers also represent another group of non-medical reporters of abuse when individuals identify themselves as such. These individuals use a multitude of criteria for ascertaining whether an incident represents abuse. These non-medical reporters primarily use criteria and report abuse on their personal perception of child maltreatment if they have knowledge of abuse indicators. For those reporters who rely on their personal perceptions of what constitutes abuse, the reports they make are usually based on their values and beliefs surrounding child-rearing practice and a family's right to privacy (Butz 1985; Conrad and Schneider 1980). For example, a neighbor who observes physical injury being inflicted upon a child may or may not report the incident depending on what they perceive as appropriate or inappropriate discipline; and whether they feel governmental systems have the right to intrude or not into family matters. A person's values about child-rearing, family privacy, and role of government can significantly influence whether a report is made and the types of incidents reported (Giovannoni and Becerra 1979; Gil 1979). These potential reporters' relationship to the family may cause them to rely on hearsay information in many instances (Mayhill and Norgard 1983).

To illustrate, a family friend reports an incident based on information obtained from the children's grandparent, who observed the incident but is reluctant to make a report. The reporter in this case is only able to corroborate the report upon investigation with hearsay information if the grandmother wishes to remain anonymous, which would be inadmissible in a court hearing. Therefore, if physical injury of abuse is not evident upon investigation, child protective services (CPS) investigators are unable to substantiate the report even when abuse is suspected.

Non-medical reporters in this group do, for the most part, report incidents they allegedly observed directly. These non-medical reporters are less likely than any other group of medical or non-medical reporters (i.e., physical, nurses, law enforcement officers, day care providers, social workers, etc.) to provide concrete supportive evidence such as pictures of child's injuries, x-rays, medical records, or parental confessions of abuse (Giovannoni and Becerra 1979; Mayhill and Norgard 1983). For the most part, these reporters (non-medical) often encounter incidents of abuse in settings that do not afford them access to resources that are available to medical reporters (Garbarino 1979). These reporters are, however, critical to the child abuse reporting system because they provide the CPS system with access to children and families in need of intervention who may not come to the attention of the system through reporters in formal organizations (i.e., schools, health care facilities, law enforcement departments, public/private social services, etc.).

Child abuse reporting as discussed from an ecological framework suggests that the environment of the reporters, along with their backgrounds, beliefs and values regarding child maltreatment and societal expectations influences the types of children and families that are more likely to be reported for abuse. Using the concepts presented in the literature and the tenets of the ecological perspective, the author discusses in the following chapters a study conducted on urban child abuse reporting that analyzes the differences in reporting among medical and non-medical reporters. Specifically, the study examines the following factors involved with reporting and report dispositions:

1. the differences between child abuse reporting by medical and non-medical sources in relationship to the characteristics of children, families and perpetrators they report; and
2. the differences between the rate of report substantiation and unsubstantiation for child abuse reporting by medical and non-medical sources.

Part Two

Urban Child Abuse Reporting Study

IV

Urban Child Abuse Reporting:
The Study Methodology

INTRODUCTION

In Part II of this book the author presents a study of urban child abuse reporting that focuses on medical and non-medical reporting sources. This study describes the differences in report characteristics that these reporters make known. Because child abuse reporting does not end once a report is made, this study further examines the differences in dispositions rendered to reports from medical and non-medical sources. The chapters in this section discuss the study in depth.

This chapter presents the methodology used in studying urban medical and non-medical child abuse reporting. The reporting laws for the study site are reviewed as a framework for understanding the kinds of reporters and the different settings generating reports of suspected child abuse for investigation. Study objectives are defined, and a detailed description of the measurement of urban child abuse reporting and report dispositions are discussed. Finally, the procedures are presented for sampling, data collection and data analysis.

STUDY SITE REPORTING LAWS

This study examines child abuse reporting in the urban area of Baltimore City, Maryland. Maryland's child abuse reporting laws are similar to most states (See Appendix A Maryland Child Abuse Reporting Laws and Statistics). The Maryland law requires health practitioners, police officers, educators, and human services workers acting in a professional capacity, who have reason to believe that a child has been abused or neglected, to notify the local department of social services or the appropriate law enforcement agency. Educators include teachers, school administrators, and counselors. Human services workers include social workers, case workers, and probation or parole officers, (Subtitle 7 Maryland Family Law Code Annotated July 1988; Subtitle 7 Maryland's Civil Child Abuse and Neglect Law October 1994). This legislative policy also provides immunity from any civil liability or criminal penalty to any person who in good faith makes or participates in making a report of abuse or neglect, participates in an investigation, or participates in a resulting judicial proceeding. While Maryland requires that professionals report suspected maltreatment, it does not have a legislatively mandated sanction for non-reporting.

The Maryland law defines an abused child as a person under the age of 18 years who has sustained physical or mental injury as a result of a malicious act or acts, or was sexually abused, meaning an act or acts involving sexual molestation or exploitation whether physical injuries are sustained or not, by parent, adoptive parent, or other persons who have the permanent or temporary care, custody or responsibility for supervision of a minor child (Maryland Department of Human Resources 1989; Subtitle 7 Maryland's Civil Child Abuse and Neglect Law October 1994).

Maryland law emphasizes two factors as determinants that abuse has indeed occurred:

1. the child suffered physical injury, or sexual abuse or exploitation with or without injury; and
2. the injury was caused non-accidentally by, or sexual abuse was perpetrated by, a person who had care, custody, or supervision of the child at the time (Subtitle 7 Maryland's Civil Child Abuse and Neglect Law October 1994).

STUDY DESIGN

This study of Urban Medical and Non-Medical Child Abuse Reporting was designed to examine the report characteristics and case dispositions for medical and non-medical reports. The objective of the study is to determine the differences in reporting among these reporting sources. Because the manifestation of physical and sexual abuse are different, reports are analyzed separately and in combination. The questions addressed by the study are:

1. Do reports of suspected child abuse from medical and non-medical reporting sources differ in relationship to the reported demographic characteristics of the alleged child abuse victims, their families, and the alleged perpetrators?
2. Do reports of suspected child abuse from medical and non-medical reporting sources differ in relationship to the type and severity of injury sustained by the alleged child abuse victims?
3. Does the rate of substantiation and unsubstantiation differ for reports of suspected child abuse from medical and non-medical reporting sources.

These study questions were further operationalized as hypotheses to provide a framework for analyzing outcomes. First, it is hypothesized that the reported characteristics of alleged child abuse incidents are related to the reporting source. It is predicted that medical reporting sources more often report young, black, male children who sustain visible physical injury or specific sexual abuse, young caretakers, mothers/mother substitutes as perpetrators, and families who reside in poverty areas compared to non-medical reporting sources. It is further predicted that non-medical reporting sources more often report older, white and other race, female children who sustain non-visible physical injury or no specific sexual abuse, older caretakers, fathers/father substitutes and other individuals as perpetrators, and families who reside in non-poverty areas compared to medical reporting sources.

Second, it is hypothesized that the dispositions of suspected child abuse reports are related to the reporting source. It is predicted that reports from medical reporting sources are more often substantiated than reports from non-medical reporting sources. It is further predicted that reports from non-medical reporting sources are more often unsubstantiated than reports from medical sources.

MEASURES

Conceptualizing Child Abuse Reporting

The measures for this study were structured according to the design stated and explores four aspects of child abuse reporting: characteristics of the child abuse incidents, disposition, suspected child abuse reports, and reporting sources. The definitions are:

Characteristics of the Child Abuse Incidents connote the demographics of the alleged child abuse victims, their families and alleged perpetrators; and the severity of the alleged victim's injury as enumerated in the child abuse reporting literature.

Disposition identifies the determination made by CPS practitioners denoting whether sufficient evidence exists to support or reject the occurrence of child abuse.

Suspected Child Abuse Reports refers to those child abuse incidents reported to the local child welfare authorities for investigation.

Reporting Sources refers to those mandated and non-mandated persons in the community who make known to the local child welfare authorities suspected incidents of child abuse.

Operationalizing Child Abuse Reporting

Child abuse reporting was operationalized using the following nominal level measures:

Characteristics of the Child Abuse Incidents include physical abuse allegations; sexual abuse allegations; age, race, and sex of children; age of caretakers; alleged perpetrators; and socio-economic status of families' areas of residence as reported in suspected child abuse reports made to the local child welfare authorities. The characteristics are subdivided into the following operational categories.

1. *Physical Abuse Allegations* were determined based on the physical injury to the alleged child(ren) in the report. This variable

was classified into the categories: a) no visible injury, and b) visible injury. No visible injury included reports stating the child was beaten, punched, slapped, or bitten even though no injury was evident. Visible injury included reports stating the child had bruises, cuts, abrasions, burns, contusions, fractures, internal injuries, was poisoned, or died.

2. *Sexual Abuse Allegations* were determined based on the sexual abuse sustained by the child(ren) as stated in the report. This variable was classified into the categories: a) no specific sexual act, and b) specific sexual act. No specific sexual act included reports that implied the child had a venereal disease, sexual tickling, child is encouraged, pressured, or propositioned to perform sexual acts but no sexual activity or molestation occurred, and sexual exhibitionism implied. Specific sexual act included reports that stated one or more of the following acts took place, such as touching/ fondling of genitals or breast (maybe mutual, digital intercourse, oral intercourse, fellation or cunnilingus, anal intercourse, and genital intercourse).

3. *Age of Children* is the age of the child(ren) indicated in the alleged child abuse reports. This variable was classified into the categories: a) young children covers infancy to 9 years, and b) older children, ages 10 to 17 years.

4. *Race of Children* was determined based on the race indicated in the report. This variable was classified into the categories: a) black, b) white, and c) others (i.e., Hispanic, Native American, Asian/Pacific Islanders, bi-racial, and other racial groups not recognized as blacks or whites).

5. *Sex of Children* was determined based on the gender stated in the report for the alleged abused child(ren). The categories include: a) males, and b) females.

6. *Age of Caretaker* was based on the age of the parent or guardian, as stated in the report, with whom the allegedly abused child(ren) lived, and who had responsibility to provide for the care of the child(ren) at the time of the report. This variable was classified into the categories a) young caretakers, ages 15 to 24 years, and b) older caretakers, ages 25 years and older.

7. *Alleged Perpetrator* is the person alleged in the report as physically or sexually abusing the child(ren). The categories are:

a) mothers/mother substitutes (biological mother, foster mother, stepmother, and father's paramour), b) father/father substitutes (biological father, foster father, stepfather, and mother's paramour, and c) other individuals (other female/male relatives, female/male non-relatives, school/professional child care providers, and non-professional baby-sitters).

8. *Socio-Economic Status (SES) of Families' Areas of Residence* is the determination of whether the reported families lived in: a) non-poverty area, or b) poverty area. The SES of reported families' residence was based on the census tract in which they lived as stated in the reports. The determination of a non-poverty or poverty area was based on the 1980 U. S. census data reflecting the percentage of families with children who lived below poverty in a given census tract.

Disposition was based on the outcome of the investigation of the report. In Maryland, at the time the data were collected, the possible outcomes were confirmed, indicated, uncertain, or ruled out (See Appendix A: Maryland Child Abuse Reporting Law Definitions of Dispositions). These outcomes were collapsed and dichotomized into substantiated and unsubstantiated. Substantiated reports included those determined by the CPS investigators as confirmed or indicated for child abuse. Unsubstantiated reports were those determined as uncertain or ruled out for child abuse.

Suspected Child Abuse Reports was operationalized using the categories: a) reports of physical child abuse and b) reports of sexual abuse. Physical child abuse reports included alleged incidents of physical injury sustained by the child non-accidentally resulting from malicious acts perpetrated while in the care of parents or others having permanent or temporary responsibility or supervision of the child. Sexual child abuse reports included alleged incidents suggesting the child was sexually molested or exploited while in the care of a parent or others having permanent or temporary responsibility or supervision of the child.

Reporting Sources was determined based on where the report was generated. This variable was classified into the categories: a) medical reporting sources, and b) non-medical reporting sources. Medical reporting sources were operationalized to include any health care facility professional staff (physicians, nurses, social workers, therapists, etc.) making a report of alleged child abuse to the local child protective services agency for investigation. Health care facilities included acute, chronic, and mental hospitals as well as their out-patient clinics; family planning clinics; well-baby clinics; private health practitioners' offices; and local and state health departments. Non-medical reporting sources included personnel in public social services agencies, private social services agencies, public housing authorities, schools, child care facilities, law enforcement agencies, juvenile services agencies; and neighbors, friends, victims, relatives, biological/adoptive parents, foster parents, stepparents, and anonymous callers identified as such in reports of alleged child abuse made to the local CPS agency for investigation.

METHODOLOGY

Child Abuse Report Sample

A sample of 576 alleged child abuse reports were randomly selected from the 1984 Child Abuse Report and Disposition File of the Baltimore City Department of Social Services (BCDSS) Child Protective Services Unit. The file consists of 2870 alleged child abuse reports made to the BCDSS Child Protective Services Unit during the calendar year January 1 through December 31, 1984. To be included in the sampling frame a report had to meet the general study criteria that the alleged abuse was physical or sexual, a report disposition was rendered, and the report was generated by a urban medical or non-medical reporting source. To ensure randomization of the sample, case numbers were used in a random numbers procedure to construct the sample.

Data Collection

The data collected for this study was drawn from the study sample of alleged child abuse reports. Data collected was descriptive and represented nominal level measures. To ensure consistency in the collection of data, a codebook and schedule were used (See Appendix B Codebook and Schedule for Urban Medical and Non-Medical Reports). All the data from reports in the sample were coded onto the coding schedule. The codebook and schedule were pre-tested.

Data was collected by coders trained on the codebook and schedule. Each coder was responsible for obtaining data from 192 reporters. Quality control procedures included requiring a random selection of 50 percent of each coder's reports to be re-coded by another coder to maintain consistency in the data collection process.

Data Analysis

Data analysis of alleged child abuse reports were conducted according to the reporting source—medical and non-medical reporters—to determine if differences exist as predicted by these reports. Reports from each category of reporters were analyzed by characteristics of children, their families, alleged perpetrators, alleged abuse, and report disposition. Separate and combined analysis of the type of alleged abuse, physical or sexual, were also undertaken according to the reporting source of the report.

Analysis was carried out using the significance of the difference between proportions and chi-square statistics. The difference between proportions formula used is:

$$z = \frac{p1 - p2}{\sqrt{\frac{p1q1}{n1} + \frac{p2q2}{n2}}}$$

p1 = proportion of medical reporting sources.
p2 = proportion of non-medical reporting sources.
q1 = 1 - p1.
q2 = 1 - p2.
n1 = number of reports from medical reporting sources.
n2 = number of reports from non-medical reporting sources.

The significance of the difference between proportions statistically analyzed the relationship between the stated measures in the study reflecting dichotomized classifications. Chi-square was used to analyze the relationship between measures consisting of more than two classifications. The significance level for the tests was set at $p < .05$. It is important to recognize that when conducting several tests the probability of finding statistical differences where there are none increases. Thus, these statistics are used because of their utility to determine whether systematic relationships exist.

Given the limited state of the current knowledge pertaining to examining the differences in characteristics and dispositions of medical and non-medical reports, this approach is exploratory in nature. And, the findings must be interpreted with caution due to the limited sample population, and should be recognized as descriptive.

V

Urban Child Abuse Reporting:
The Study Sample

This chapter presents the characteristics of the alleged abused children, their families, perpetrators, and reporting sources in this study sample.

DESCRIPTION OF THE SAMPLE

Age of Reported Children

The study sample includes 671 children reported for abuse. Ages were not reported for 39 of the alleged children in this study. Reported children range in age from one month to 17 years. Ages of the children are grouped into two categories: 1) young children from infancy to 9 years, and 2) older children of 10 to 17 years. Table 5.1 indicates 64.1% (405) of the children are infants to 9 years, and 35.9% (227) are aged 10 to 17 years. The mean age for younger children is 5 years, and for older children 14 years. The overall mean age for the children in the sample is 8 years. Young children appear to be the most often reported.

Several factors may, at least in part explain the over-representation of young children from infancy to 9 years. Young children, especially those 5 years and younger, demand almost continuous physical and emotional attention (Fontana 1973; Maden 1980; Jason et al. 1982; Lindsey 1994). These children are less mobile and more fragile. Consequently, they are the population more likely to sustain a serious injury from an assault which comes to the attention of child welfare authorities (Fontana 1973; Jason et al. 1982; Ditson and Shay 1984). Whereas, an assault against older children

may be regarded as an accidental injury and not brought to the attention of
child welfare authorities (Johnson and Shower 1985; Ditson and Shay 1984;
Farber and Joseph 1985; Lindsey 1994).

	TABLE 5.1	
	Ages of Reported Children	
Ages*	Percent	Number
Infancy to 9 years	64.1	405
10 years to 17 years	35.9	227
Total	100.0	632
*Ages unknown = 39 (5.8% of the total 671 children reported)		

Race of Reported Children

Table 5.2 indicates 70.4% (407) of the reported children in the sample are
black, 26.8% (155) white, and 2.8% (16) from other racial groups. Race is
unknown for 93 children.

	TABLE 5.2	
	Race of Reported Children	
Race*	Percent	Number
Black	70.4	407
White	26.8	155
Others	2.8	16
Total	100.0	578
*Race unknown = 93 (13.9% of the total 671 children reported)		

The 1980 census statistics for Baltimore indicate that the racial
breakdown for the population from infancy to 17 years included 67% black,
31.7% white, and 1.3% others. From the census statistics it appears that the
study sample is approximately representative of the population of children
from infancy to 17 years in Baltimore. While black children comprise the
largest group of children reported for abuse in 1984, this occurrence may be
attributed to the majority racial status they represent in Baltimore according

to the 1980 census. This occurrence could also mean black children are reported more often for abuse due to reporter bias.

Sex of Reported Children

Table 5.3 indicates that 42.3% (284) of the reported children were male while 57.7% (387) of the reported children were females.

TABLE 5.3		
Sex of Reported Children		
Sex	Percent	Number
Male	42.3	284
Female	57.7	387
Total	100.0	671

The 1980 Baltimore City census statistics indicated that of the population from infancy to 17 years female children represent 49%, and male children represent 51%. The census data reflected that males comprise 2% more of the city's population from infancy to 17 years than females. The study sample indicates, however, that 15.4% more female children were reported for abuse than male children. The difference between female and male children reported in this study is statistically significant ($p < .05$, $z = 3.51$).

Such differences in the reporting of male and female children for abuse have been attributed to the high incidence of female children being reported for sexual abuse. According to the U.S. Department of Health and Human Services (1995); Pierce and Pierce (1985); Finkelhor (1980); and Geiser (1979) reporters view sexual abuse as acts primarily directed toward female children, and physical abuse as acts perpetrated against male and female children almost equally depending on the age of the child. These studies suggest that female children are more likely to be the majority group reported for abuse because they are alleged twice as often as victims of sexual abuse, and also constitute a significant segment of the victims reported for physical abuse (U.S. Department of Health and Human Services 1995; Pierce and Pierce 1985; Finkelhor 1980; Geiser 1979).

This sample indicates also that female children are reported for sexual abuse substantially more frequently than male children. It further shows that male and female children are reported at almost the same percentage for physical abuse. To illustrate, of the 205 sexual abuse allegations made in this sample, males represent 7.5% (14), and females 92.5% (191). And, for the 474 physical abuse allegations made, males represent 54.9% (261) and females 45.1% (213).

The high rate of reporting female children as victims of sexual abuse contributed to their majority status in this study. But it can not be concluded from this study if this phenomenon in reporting is a result of reporter bias, or whether female children are indeed abused more often than male children, regardless of type of abuse.

Age of Reported Caretakers

Five hundred seventy-six caretakers are represented in this study. Ages were not reported for 36 caretakers. The caretakers range in age from 15 to 70 years. The ages of caretakers were grouped into two categories: 1) young caretakers of 15 to 24 years; and 2) older caretakers of 25 years and older. Table 5.4 indicates 29.4% (159) of the caretakers are 15 to 24 years of age, and 70.6% (381) are 25 years and older. The mean age for caretakers 15 to 24 is 21. The mean age for caretakers 25 years and older is 34.

TABLE 5.4
Age of Reported Caretakers

Ages*	Percent	Number
15 years to 24 years	29.4	159
25 years to 70 years	70.6	381
Total	100.0	540

*Ages unknown = 36 (6.3% of the total 576 caretakers reported)

Caretakers aged 25 to 70 years represent the largest group reported in this sample. Of this group of caretakers 88.4% (337) are from 25 to 40 years. The next largest groups are those aged 41 to 56 years representing 9.5% (36), and from 57 to 70 representing 2.1% (8).

The older caretakers represent the largest group in this study. This finding differed from other research (Morris et al. 1985; Maden 1980). Morris et al. (1985) found that individuals younger than 25 years, particularly biological parents, were more frequently identified in child abuse reports than caretakers 25 years of age and older.

Even though previous research suggest that younger biological parents are identified as caretakers more frequently in abuse reports, this study sample differs in that older biological parents and older extended family members (i.e., aunts, uncles, and grandparents) are the caretakers more often reported. Older biological parents and extended family members aged 25 years and older represent 60% (324) of the caretakers reported. The remaining older caretakers include foster and step parents representing 10.6% (57). Older caretakers in this study represent a much broader population of individuals reported as caretakers in comparison to those reported as younger caretakers. The category of young caretakers only include biological parents, which indeed represents a limited scope of possible caretakers. Essentially, the over-representation of older caretakers in the study sample is attributed to the diversity of individuals reported in this category as caretakers.

Alleged Perpetrators

There were 605 alleged perpetrators identified in the study. The alleged perpetrator(s) were missing for 73 reported children. The alleged perpetrators are grouped into three categories: 1) mothers/mother substitutes, 2) fathers/father substitutes, and 3) others. Table V indicates mothers/mother substitutes comprised 45.1% (273), fathers/father substitutes comprised 35.9% (217), and other comprised 19.0% (115) of the study sample. Mothers/mother substitutes represent the largest category of alleged perpetrators in this study.

	TABLE 5.5	
	Alleged Perpetrators	
Alleged Perpetrators*	Percent	Number
Mothers/Mother Substitutes	45.1	273
Fathers/Father Substitutes	35.9	217
Others	19.0	115
Total	100.0	605

*Alleged perpetrators unknown = 73 (10.8% of the total 678 perpetrators reported)

Further breakdown of these categories reflect that biological mothers (42.6%), and biological fathers (20.5%) represent the most frequently alleged perpetrators of child abuse. (See Table 5.6).

	TABLE 5.6	
	Individual Classifications of Alleged Perpetrators	
Individual Classifications of Alleged Perpetrators	Percent	Number
Biological Mothers	42.6	258
Female Relatives	4.1	25
Female Non-Professionals		
Baby-sitters	2.3	14
Foster Mothers	1.8	11
Female School Professionals		
Day Care Providers	0.5	3
Stepmothers	0.3	2
Fathers' Paramours	0.3	2
Female Non-Relatives	0.2	1
Biological Fathers	20.5	124
Mothers' Paramours	9.8	59
Male Relatives	6.9	42
Stepfathers	5.6	34
Male Non-Relatives	2.7	16
Male Non-Professionals		

TABLE 5.6 (cont.)		
Baby-sitters	1.7	10
Male School/Professionals		
Day Care Providers	0.7	4
Foster Fathers	0.0	0
Total	100.0	605

According to studies conducted by Hampton and Newberger (1985); Ditson and Shay (1984); and Zuravin and Starr (1991) mothers are the most often alleged perpetrators of physical abuse. These authors suggest that two critical factors account for mothers being the most often alleged perpetrators of physical child abuse. First, mothers are more frequently the primary caretaker, which includes the ongoing responsibility for disciplining the child. In most cases of physical abuse the mother's abusive actions toward the child results from disciplinary measures taken to control the child (Ditson and Shay 1984; Zuravin and Starr 1991).

Mothers (i.e., biological, foster, step and father's paramour) in this study represented 55% (297) of the caretakers reported. Forty-one percent of the mothers identified as caretakers, with whom the child resides, were also the alleged abusers of physical child abuse.

The second factor accounting for the high incidence of mothers alleged as abusers is they are most often reported for the leading type of child abuse (physical abuse) (Hampton and Newberger 1985; Johnson and Showers 1985, Zuravin and Starr 1991). In this study on urban child abuse reporting, physical abuse allegations constituted 69.8% (474) of the reports. Mothers/mother substitutes were alleged as perpetrators in 60.9%3 (246) of the physical abuse reports (See Table 5.7). It appears from this sample that mothers/mother substitutes are more often the alleged perpetrators of physical abuse largely because of their role in the child's life, which gives them greater access to the child.

Fathers/father substitutes are recognized as the second largest perpetrators of child physical abuse. Gil (1979, 1975, 1970); Giovannoni and Becerra (1979); and Mayhill and Norgard (1983) suggest that fathers/father substitutes constitute such a significant group of perpetrators in physical abuse reports largely because they are most often the perpetrators of domestic physical violence, which quite frequently results in not only abuse against the spouse/paramour but also the child(ren). In this study the author found biological, adoptive, foster, and step fathers represent 30% (165) of the caretakers reported. Twelve percent of fathers identified as caretakers, with whom the child resides, were also labeled as perpetrators of child physical abuse. Father/father substitutes constituted 21.8% (88) of the alleged perpetrators of physical child abuse (See Table 5.7).

Other individuals identified represent 17.3% (70) of the perpetrators for child physical abuse in this study (See Table 5.7). Mayhill and Norgard (1983) suggest that other individuals as a group of alleged perpetrators are the least frequently reported largely because their access to the children is not as great as the parents, when they are not the caretaker with whom the child resides. Further breakdown of this category of alleged perpetrators indicates that females represent 67.7% (46) and males 34.3% (24) of the perpetrators of child physical abuse.

TABLE 5.7
Alleged Perpetrators of Physical Child Abuse

Alleged Perpetrators	Percent	Number
Mothers/Mother Substitutes	60.9	246
Fathers/Father Substitutes	21.8	88
Other Individuals	17.3	70
Total	100.0	404

Father/father substitutes represent the most often alleged perpetrators of child sexual abuse (Pierce and Pierce 1985; Tyler 1984; Geiser 1979; Herman and Hirschman 1977). Even though, fathers/father substitutes represent the leading perpetrators of sexual abuse they are still ranked second to mothers/mother substitutes in the overall population of alleged perpetrators of child abuse. This ranking exists because mothers/mother substitutes are more often reported for physical abuse, the nation's leading reported type of abuse.

In this study sexual abuse allegations represent 30.2% (205) of the reports. Table 5.8 indicates fathers/father substitutes in this study represent 54.2% (109) of alleged perpetrators reported for sexual abuse. Mother/mother substitutes comprise 23.4% (47) of the alleged perpetrators of sexual abuse. Taylor (1984) suggest that many instances of sexual abuse by mothers/mother substitutes is between male adolescents, and father's paramours or stepmothers. In contrast, this study, indicates biological mothers were the leading perpetrators of sexual abuse with male children.

Other individuals comprise 22.4% (45) of reported perpetrators. Studies conducted by Glaser and Frosh (1988); Burnley (1986); Finkelhor (1980, 1984) suggest other male individuals (i.e., relatives, non-relatives, school/professional day care providers) are a recognizably growing population of perpetrators that are being reported for sexual abuse. This study indicates that other male individuals represent 77.8% (35) of the alleged perpetrators reported for sexual abuse, while females in this category represented 22.2% (10). Vander Mey and Neff (1986); and Pierce and Pierce (1985) suggest that the increased identification of various perpetrators of sexual child abuse is a result of the growing recognition of incest as child abuse in our society. Essentially, the study sample supports the existing literature that the majority status of a particular group alleged as perpetrators is related to the type of child abuse perpetrated against children.

TABLE 5.8
Alleged Perpetrators of Sexual Child Abuse

Alleged Perpetrator	Percent	Number
Mothers/Mother Substitutes	23.4	47
Fathers/Mother Substitutes	54.2	109
Other Individuals	22.4	45
Total	100.0	201

Reported Families' Areas of Residence

The study sample includes 576 reported families. The reported families' areas of residence were grouped into two categories: 1) families residing in non-poverty areas; and 2) families residing in poverty areas. Table 5.9 indicates the reported families residing in non-poverty areas comprise 27.1% (156), and families residing in poverty areas comprise 72.9% (420) of this study sample. From this breakdown the majority of reported families reside in poverty areas.

TABLE 5.9
Reported Families' Areas of Residence

Reported Families' Areas of Residence	Percent	Number
Non-Poverty Areas	27.1	156
Poverty Areas	72.9	420
Total	100.0	576

The over-representation of reported families residing in poverty areas in this study can be explained in relation to the geographic location of the reporters and reported families. McDonald and Reece (1979) and Lindsey (1994) suggest that reporting of low-income families is higher in the inner-city where a concentrated number of low income families reside. Hence, these families are more vulnerable to being reported by inner-city institutions and other members of the community.

Therefore, because of the high concentration of low income families in Baltimore City residing in poverty areas within the catchment boundaries of both medical and non-medical reporting sources in this study, the sample seems to reflect previous research regarding the geographic location of reporters and the reporting of low-income families. From this study sample it appears that geographic location does have an impact on the reporting patterns of abuse for inner city reporting sources.

Reporting Sources

The study sample included 576 child abuse reporting sources located in Baltimore City. Table 5.10 indicates medical reporting sources comprise 41.1% (237) of the study sample, and non-medical reporting sources comprise 58.9% (339). In order of frequency the following reporting sources were identified: 1) medical facilities 41.1% (237); neighbors, friends, victims, parents, and other relatives 24.8% (143); anonymous callers 10.1% (58), public social services agencies 8.7% (50); schools/day care facilities 7.5% (43); other professional agencies, i.e., law enforcement, juvenile services, and private social services, 7.5% (43); and public housing projects 0.3% (2).

TABLE 5.10
Reporting Sources

Reporting Sources	Percent	Number
Medical Reporting Sources	41.1	237
Non-Medical Reporting Sources	58.9	339
Total	100.0	576

Of the medical reporting sources identified, Johns Hopkins Hospital represents 27.0% (64), University of Maryland Hospital 21.9% (52), and Sinai Hospital 7.6% (18). These hospital systems at the time of this study comprised individually the largest number of reports generated mainly due to their extensive catchment areas in relationship to other health systems in the city. The remaining hospitals in Baltimore during 1984 comprise together 33.3% (79). Other health care facilities comprise 9.7% (23), and private practitioners 0.4% (1) of the reporters in this study (See Table 5.11).

TABLE 5.11
Categories of Medical Reporting Sources

Medical Reporting Sources	Percent	Number
Johns Hopkins Hospital	27.0	64
University of Maryland Hospital	21.9	52
Sinai Hospital	7.6	18
*Remaining Hospitals in Baltimore	33.3	79
**Other Health Care Facilities	9.7	23
Private Practitioners	0.4	1
Total	100.0	237

*Mercy, Union Memorial, Wyman Park Public Health, Greater Baltimore Medical Center, North Charles General, Baltimore City, Maryland General, South Baltimore General Good Samaritan, Lutheran, Provident, and St. Agnes Hospitals.
**Walter P. Carter Center, Health Maintenance Organizations, Community Health Nurses, Community Medical Plans, Public Departments of Health, Planned Parenthood, etc.

Of the non-medical reporting sources identified, neighbors, friends, victims, parents and other relatives comprise 42.2% (143); anonymous callers 17.1% (58), public social services agencies 14.7% (50), schools/day care facilities and other professional agencies each comprise 12.7% (43), and public housing projects 0.6% (2), see Table 5.12. Mayhill and Norgard (1983) suggest that neighbors, friends, parents, and other relatives are often frequent reporters of abuse because of the informal relationships they maintain with the alleged abused child(ren) and family, which affords them in many instances direct insight into the level of dysfunction within the family system.

TABLE 5.12
Categories of Non-Medical Reporting Sources

Non-Medical Reporting Sources	Percent	Number
Neighbors, Friends, Victims, Parents, and Other Relatives	42.2	143
Anonymous Callers	17.1	58
Public Social Services Agencies	14.7	50
Schools/Day Care Facilities	12.7	43
Other Professional Agencies	12.7	43
Public Housing Projects	0.6	2
Total	100.0	339

VI

Urban Child Abuse Reporting:
The Study Findings

This study on Urban Medical and Non-Medical Child Abuse Reporting focuses on determining to what extent are the characteristics of alleged child abuse reports and the dispositions of suspected reports related to the reporting sources. Findings are presented according to the study hypothesis with the results for physical and sexual abuse reports presented in combination and separately. First, the analysis of the differences in medical and non-medical child abuse reports is presented. Specifically, in this analysis the reported characteristics of children, their families, and the alleged perpetrators and abuse allegation are discussed. Second, the differences between report dispositions of substantiated and unsubstantiated child abuse are analyzed for reports from medical and non-medical reporting sources.

REPORTING SOURCES
AND REPORTED CHARACTERISTICS

It is predicted for this study that reports from medical reporting sources compared to reports from non-medical reporting sources are more likely to indicate one or more of the following characteristics: 1) children with visible physical injury or with a specific sexual act perpetrated against them; 2) young children; 3) black children; 4) male children; 5) children whose caretakers are young; 6) mothers/mother substitutes alleged as perpetrators; or 7) families residing in poverty areas. It is further predicted that reports from non-medical reporting source compared to reports from medical

reporting sources are more likely to indicate one or more of the following
characteristics: 1) children with no visible physical injuries who also had no
specific sexual acts perpetrated against them; 2) older children; 3) white and
other race children; 4) female children; 5) children whose caretakers are
older; 6) fathers/father substitutes and other individuals alleged as
perpetrators; or 7) families residing in non-poverty areas.

Combined Analysis

The combined analysis of physical and sexual abuse reports indicate medical
reporting sources and non-medical reporting sources are statistically
different (p<.05) as predicted for the characteristics of physical abuse
allegations, age of reported children, race of reported children, and reported
families' areas of residence. Medical and non-medical reports are not
statistically different, as illustrated in Table 6.1, for the characteristics of
sexual abuse allegations, sex of reported children, and age of reported
caretakers.

TABLE 6.1
DIFFERENCE BETWEEN PROPORTIONS OF REPORTING
SOURCES BY CHARACTERISTICS FOR PHYSICAL AND
SEXUAL ABUSE REPORTS

Variables	* p1 - p2	z Score	Significance
Physical Abuse Allegations/ Reporting Sources	.767-.491=.276	6.13	*
Sexual Abuse Allegations/ Reporting Sources	.579-.671=.092	-1.35	NS
Age of Reported Children/ Reporting Sources	.750-.570=.180	4.86	*
Sex of Reported Children/ Reporting Sources	.432-.418=.014	0.359	NS
Age of Reported Children/ Reporting Sources	.391-.280=.039	0.951	NS
Families' Areas of Residence/ Reporting Sources.	.789-.687=.102	2.76	*

---

*   Indicates statistical significance as predicted at p.<.05.
**   p1 = proportion for medical reporting sources.
      p2 = proportion for non-medical reporting sources.

The relationship between reporting sources and alleged perpetrators as indicated in Table 6.2 show a statistical difference, but the difference was not as predicted for this study.

TABLE 6.2
CHI-SQUARE STATISTICS FOR REPORTING SOURCES BY
REPORT CHARACTERISTICS OF PHYSICAL
AND SEXUAL ABUSE REPORTS

Variables	DF	x^2	Significance	n
Race of Reported Children/				
Reporting Sources	2	30.351	p.<.05	578
*Alleged Perpetrators/				
Reporting Sources	2	23.952	p.<.05	605

*Relationship between reporting sources and alleged perpetrators is not as predicted.

It was predicted that medical reporting sources would more often report mother/mother substitutes as perpetrators compared to non-medical report sources, and non-medical reporting sources would more often report fathers/father substitutes and other individuals as perpetrator compared to medical reporting sources.

Physical and sexual abuse reports indicate differences in report characteristics between medical and non-medical reporting sources. Medical sources more often reported children with visible physical injuries (76.7%), younger children (75.0%), black children (83.6%), others as perpetrators (28.7%), and families residing in poverty areas (78.9%) compared to non-medical sources. Non-medical sources reported fewer children with visible physical injuries (49.1%), young children (57.0%), black children (62.3%), others as perpetrators (13.9%), and families residing in poverty areas (68.7%) compared to medical sources. In contrast, non-medical sources reported more often children with no visible physical injuries (50.9%), older

children (43.0%); white (33.85) and other race (3.9%) children; mothers/
mother substitutes as perpetrators (50.8%); and families who resided in non-
poverty areas (31.3%) compared to medical sources. Medical sources
reported fewer children with no visible physical injuries (23.3%), older
children (25.0%); white (15.5%) and other race (0.9%) children; mothers/
mother substitutes (34.5%), and families residing in non-poverty areas
(21.1%) compared to non-medical sources as presented in Table 6.3. Even
though alleged perpetrators achieved statistical significance the findings
were not as predicted.

TABLE 6.3
REPORTING SOURCES BY REPORT CHARACTERISTICS FOR
PHYSICAL AND SEXUAL CHILD ABUSE REPORTS

Physical Abuse Allegations n = 474				
Reporting Sources	% No Visible Injury	% Visible Injury	Total	n
Medical	23.3	76.7	30.8	146
Non-Medical	50.9	49.1	69.2	328
Total	42.4	57.6	100.0	474

Sexual Abuse Allegations* n = 204				
Reporting Sources	% No Specific Act	% Specific Act	Total	n
Medical	42.1	57.9	55.6	114
Non-Medical	33.0	67.0	44.4	91
Total	38.0	62.0	100.0	205

Age of Reported Children n = 632				
Reporting Sources	% Young	% Older	Total	n
Medical	75.0	25.0	39.2	248
Non-Medical	57.0	43.0	60.8	384
Total	64.1	35.9	100.0	632

TABLE 6.3 (cont.)				
Race of Reported Children				
n = 578				
Reporting Sources	% Black	% White	% Others	Total	n
Medical	83.6	15.5	0.9	38.1	220
Non-Medical	62.3	33.8	3.9	61.9	358
Total	70.4	26.8	2.8	100.0	578

Sex of Reported Children*			
n = 671			
Reporting Sources	% Male	% Female	Total	n
Medical	43.2	56.8	38.3	257
Non-Medical	41.8	58.2	61.7	414
Total	42.3	57.7	100.0	671

Age of Reported Caretakers*			
n = 540			
Reporting Sources	% Young	% Older	Total	n
Medical	31.9	68.1	37.8	204
Non-Medical	28.0	72.0	62.2	336
Total	29.5	70.5	100.0	540

Alleged Perpetrators**				
n = 605				
Reporting Sources	% Mothers/ Substitutes	% Fathers/ Substitutes	% Others	Total	n
Medical	34.5	36.8	28.7	34.5	209
Non-Medical	50.8	35.3	13.9	65.5	396
Total	45.1	35.9	19.0	100.0	605

TABLE 6.3 (cont.)				
Reported Families' Areas of Residence n = 576				
Reporting Sources	% Non-Poverty Areas	% Poverty Areas	Total	n
Medical	21.1	78.9	41.2	237
Non-Medical	31.3	68.7	58.8	339
Total	27.1	72.9	100.0	576

*A statistically significant difference (p.<.05) in reporting between medical and non-medical sources was not found.

**A statistically significant difference (p.<.05) in reporting between medical and non-medical sources was indicated, but the difference did not reflect the predicted relationship stated for this study. It was predicted that medical reporting sources would more often report mothers/mothers substitutes as perpetrators, and non-medical reporting sources would more often report father/father substitutes and other individuals as perpetrators.

From these findings for the relationships between the reporting sources and the characteristics of physical abuse allegations, age of reported children, race of reported children and reported families' areas of residence indicate significant differences (p.<.05) in reporting and represented the predicted relationships as stated in the beginning of this chapter. The relationships between the reporting sources and the characteristics of sexual abuse allegations, sex of reported children, and age of caretakers were not found significant at p.<.05. Further findings indicate the relationship between reporting sources and alleged perpetrator was not as predicted.

Because physical abuse and sexual abuse are viewed as distinctly different types of child maltreatment, this study further investigates the relationships between report characteristics and reporting sources by partitioning the reports by type of child abuse, physical and sexual. This analysis was undertaken to determine is the relationship between reported characteristics and reporting sources influenced by the type of abuse.

Physical Abuse Reports

Physical abuse reports indicate medical and non-medical reporting sources are statistically different (p.<.05) as predicted in relationship to the report characteristics of physical abuse allegations, age of reported children, race of reported children, sex of reported children, and reported families areas of residence. In Table 6.4, the reports indicate medical and non-medical sources are not statistically different for the report characteristics of age of caretakers.

TABLE 6.4
DIFFERENCE BETWEEN PROPORTIONS OF REPORTING
SOURCE BY CHARACTERISTICS FOR
PHYSICAL ABUSE REPORTS

Variables	** p1 - p2	z Score	Significance
Physical Abuse Allegations/			
Reporting Sources	.767-.491=.276	6.13	*
Age of Reported Children/			
Reporting Sources	.775-.577=.198	4.30	*
Sex of Reported Children/			
Reporting Sources	.565-.456=.109	2.18	*
Age of Reported Caretakers/			
Reporting Sources	.383-.297=.086	1.62	NS
Reported Families' Areas of Residence/			
Reporting Sources	.791-.694=.097	2.20	*

* Indicates statistical significance at p.<.05.
** p1 = proportion for medical reporting sources
p2 = proportion for non-medical reporting sources

The characteristic of alleged perpetrators, as illustrated in Table 6.5, indicates a statistical difference. But it does not predict the relationship indicated in this study.

TABLE 6.5
CHI-SQUARE STATISTICS FOR REPORTING SOURCES BY
REPORT CHARACTERISTICS
FOR PHYSICAL ABUSE REPORTS

Variables	DF	x2	Significance	n
Race of Reported Children/				
Reporting Sources	2	12.326	p.<.05	409
*Alleged Perpetrators/				
Reporting Sources	2	10.024	p.<.05	416

*Relationship between reporting source and alleged perpetrators is not as predicted.

As demonstrated in Table 6.6, the findings of this study further indicate physical abuse reports differ in report characteristics for medical and non-medical reporting sources. Medical sources more often report children with visible physical injuries (76.7%), young children (77.5%), black children (78.7%), male children (56.5%), others as perpetrators (18.6%), and families residing in poverty areas (79.1%) compared to non-medical sources. Non-medical sources of physical abuse reports allege fewer children with visible physical injuries (49.1%), young children (57.7%), black children (64.2%), male children (45.6%), others as perpetrators (8.1%), and families residing in poverty areas (69.4%) compared to medical sources. In contrast, non-medical reporting sources allege more often in physical abuse reports children with no visible injuries (50.9%), older children (42.3%), white (31.5%) and other race (4.3%) children, female children (54.4%), mothers/mother substitutes (61.4%), and families residing in non-poverty areas (30.6%) compared to medical sources. Medical sources allege in physical abuse reports fewer children with no visible physical injuries (23.3%), older children (22.5%), white (21.3%) and other race (0%) children, female children (43.5%), mothers/mother substitutes as perpetrators (51.7%), and families residing in non-poverty areas (20.9%) compared to non-medical sources.

TABLE 6.6
REPORTING SOURCES BY REPORT CHARACTERISTICS FOR
PHYSICAL CHILD ABUSE REPORTS

Reporting Sources	Physical Abuse Allegations n = 474			
	% No Visible Injury	% Visible Injury	Total	n
Medical	23.3	76.7	30.8	146
Non-medical	50.9	49.1	69.2	328
Total	42.4	57.6	100.0	474

Reporting Sources	Age of Reported Children n = 431			
	% Young	% Older	Total	n
Medical	77.5	22.5	32.0	138
Non-medical	57.7	42.3	68.0	293
Total	64.0	36.0	100.0	431

Reporting Sources	Race of Reported Children n = 409				
	% Black	% White	% Others	Total	n
Medical	78.7	21.3	0.0	31.1	127
Non-Medical	64.2	31.5	4.3	68.9	282
Total	68.7	28.4	2.9	100.0	409

Reporting Sources	Sex of Reported Children n = 454			
	% Males	% Females	Total	n
Medical	56.5	43.5	31.9	145
Non-medical	45.6	54.4	68.1	309
Total	49.1	50.9	100.0	454

TABLE 6.6 (cont.)				
Age of Reported Caretakers*				
n = 383				
Reporting Sources	%	%		
	Young	Older	Total	n
Medical	38.3	61.7	31.3	120
Non-Medical	29.7	70.3	68.7	263
Total	32.4	67.6	100.0	383

Alleged Perpetrators**					
n = 416					
Reporting Sources	%	%	%		
	Mothers/	Fathers/			
	Substitutes	Substitutes	Others	Total	n
Medical	51.7	29.7	18.6	28.4	118
Non-medical	61.4	30.5	8.1	71.6	298
Total	58.6	30.3	11.1	100.0	416

Reported Families' Areas of Residence				
n = 405				
Reporting Sources	%	%		
	Non-Poverty Areas	Poverty Areas	Total	n
Medical	20.9	79.1	33.1	134
Non-medical	30.6	69.4	66.9	271
Total	27.4	72.6	100.0	405

*A statistically significant difference (p.<.05) in reporting between medical and non-medical reporting sources was not found.
**A statistically significant difference in reporting between medical and non-medial sources was indicated, but the difference did not reflect the predicted relationship stated in this study. It was predicted that medical reporting sources would more often report mothers/mother substitutes as perpetrators, and non-medical reporting sources would more often report fathers/father substitutes and other individuals as perpetrators.

Approximately the same outcomes for physical abuse reports and the combined analysis of physical and sexual abuse reports were found. The only difference was physical abuse reports indicate a significant difference in reporting between medical and non-medical sources concerning the sex of children reported. From these findings the relationships between reporting source and the report characteristics of physical abuse allegations, age of reported children, race of reported children, sex of reported children, and reported families' areas of residence indicate a significant difference (p.<.05) in reporting, and represent the predicted relationship for the study. For the report characteristic of age of caretakers no relationship was found. The relationship between reporting sources and alleged perpetrators was not as predicted.

Sexual Abuse Reports

The analysis of sexual abuse reports indicate medical and non-medical reporting sources were statistically different (p.<.05) as predicted in relationship to the report characteristics of age of reported children, race of reported children, and reported families' area of residence. As illustrated in Table 6.7, sexual abuse reports indicate medical and non-medical reporting sources were not statistically different for the report characteristics of sexual abuse allegations, sex of reported children, and age of reported caretakers.

TABLE 6.7
DIFFERENCE BETWEEN PROPORTIONS OF REPORTING
SOURCES BY CHARACTERISTICS
FOR SEXUAL ABUSE REPORTS

Variables	**p1 - p2	z Score	Significance
Sexual Abuse Allegations/			
Reporting Sources	.579-.671=.092	-1.35	NS
Age of Reported Children/			
Reporting Sources	.718-.549=.169	2.48	*
Sex of Reported Children/			
Reporting Sources	.259-.305=-.046	-0.754	NS
Age of Reported Caretakers/			

	TABLE 6.7 (cont.)	
Variables	**$p1$ - $p2$**	Score Significance
Reporting Sources	.226-.219=.007	0.105 NS
Reported Families' Area of		
Residence/ Reporting		
Sources	.786-.662=.124	1.77 *

*   Indicated statistical significance at $p<.05$.
** $p1$ = proportion for medical reporting sources.
     $p2$ = proportion for non-medical reporting sources.

For the characteristic of alleged perpetrators the relationship, as indicated in Table 6.8, was not significant.

TABLE 6.8
CHI-SQUARE STATISTICS FOR REPORTING SOURCES
BY REPORT CHARACTERISTICS
FOR SEXUAL ABUSE REPORTS

Variables	DF	$x2$	Significance	n
Race of Reported Children/				
Reporting Sources	2	30.671	$p.<.05$	169
*Alleged Perpetrators/				
Reporting Sources	2	2.871	$p.<.05$	189

*Relationship between reporting sources and alleged perpetrators is not significant.

Sexual abuse reports indicate differences in report characteristics between medical and non-medical reporting sources. In Table 6.9, medical sources more often report young children (71.8%), black children (90.3%), and families residing in poverty areas (78.6%) compared to non-medical sources. Non-medical sources allege in sexual abuse reports fewer young children (54.9%), black children (55.3%), and families residing in poverty areas (66.2%) compared to medical sources. In contrast, non-medical reporting sources allege more often in sexual abuse reports older children (45.1%), white children (42.1%), and families residing in non-poverty areas (33.8%) compared to medical sources. Medical sources allege in sexual abuse reports fewer older children (28.2%), white children (7.5%), and families residing in non-poverty areas (21.4%) compared to non-medical sources.

TABLE 6.9
REPORTING SOURCES BY REPORT CHARACTERISTICS
FOR SEXUAL ABUSE REPORTS

Reporting Sources	% No Specific Act	% Specific Act	Total	n
	Sexual Abuse Allegations* n = 205			
Medical	42.1	57.9	55.6	114
Non-Medical	33.0	67.0	44.4	91
Total	38.0	62.0	100.0	205
	Age of Reported Children n = 201			
Reporting Sources	% Young	% Older	Total	n
Medical	71.8	28.2	54.7	110
Non-Medical	54.9	45.1	45.3	91
Total	64.2	35.8	100.0	201

TABLE 6.9 (cont.)				
Race of Reported Children n = 169				
Reporting Sources	% Black	% White	% Others	Total	n
Medical	90.3	7.5	2.2	55.0	93
Non-medical	55.3	42.1	2.6	45.0	76
Total	74.5	23.1	2.4	100.0	169

Sex of Reported Children* n = 217				
Reporting Sources	% Male	% Female	Total	n
Medical	25.9	74.1	51.6	112
Non-medical	30.5	69.5	48.4	105
Total	28.1	71.9	100.0	217

Age of Reported Caretakers* n = 157				
Reporting Sources	% Young	% Older	Total	n
Medical	22.6	77.4	53.5	84
Non-medical	21.9	78.1	46.5	73
Total	22.3	77.7	100.0	157

TABLE 6.9 (cont.)					
Alleged Perpetrators*					
n = 189					
Reporting Sources %	%	%			
Mothers/Mother	Fathers/Father				
Substitutes	Substitutes	Others	Total	n	
Medical	12.1	46.1	41.8	8.2	91
Non-medical	18.4	50.0	31.6	51.8	98
Total	15.3	48.2	36.5	100.0	189
Reported Families' Areas of Residence					
n = 171					
Reporting Sources %	%				
Non-Poverty Areas	Poverty Areas		Total	n	
Medical	21.4	78.6		60.2	103
Non-medical	33.8	66.2		39.8	68
Total	26.3	73.7		100.0	171

*A statistically significant difference (p<.05) in reporting between medical and non-medical reporting sources was not found.
**A statistically significant difference (p<.05) in reporting between medical and non-medical reporting sources was indicated, but the difference was not as predicted for the study. It was predicted that medical reporting sources more often report mothers/mother substitutes as perpetrators, and non-medical reporting sources more often report fathers/father substitutes and others as perpetrators.

Sexual abuse reports indicate fewer differences in the report characteristics between medical and non-medical reporting sources. For the relationship between reporting sources and the report characteristics of age of reported children, race of reported children, and reported families' areas of residence, the findings were significant as predicted. The relationships are not significant between reporting sources and sexual abuse allegations, sex of reported children, and age of caretakers. Furthermore, findings for the relationship between reporting sources and alleged perpetrators was not as predicted in the study.

Summary of Report Characteristics

The data reports findings that medical and non-medical reporting sources differ in relationship to various report characteristics pertaining to children, their families, and alleged perpetrators. Specifically, the findings of this study indicate that medical reporting sources report a larger percentage of children who are young, black, sustain visible physical injuries, and families residing in poverty areas. While non-medical sources tend to report a larger percentage of children who are older, white and other race children, sustained less serious physical abuse, as well as families residing in non-poverty areas. For the report characteristic of alleged perpetrators from medical reporting sources, the combined analysis of physical and sexual abuse reports, and the separate analysis of physical abuse reports indicates other individuals as perpetrators are more often reported. Non-medical reporting sources reported mothers/mother substitutes more often in these groups of reports. These findings did not support the predicted relationship between reporting sources and alleged perpetrators.

REPORTING SOURCES AND REPORT DISPOSITIONS

The second part of this study discusses the dispositions of suspected child abuse reports in regard to the reporting sources. It is predicted that reports from medical reporting sources are more likely to be substantiated for child abuse, whereas reports from non-medical reporting sources are more likely to be unsubstantiated.

Combined Analysis

The combined analysis of physical and sexual abuse reports from medical and non-medical reporting sources resulted in a statistically significant difference ($p < .05$, *p1 .498 - p2 .337 = .161, z = 3.74$) in relationship to the report dispositions of substantiated and unsubstantiated. The findings indicate that medical sources (49.8%) alleged more often reports that are substantiated for abuse than non-medical source (33.7%). Non-medical sources (66.3%) more often reported incidents that are unsubstantiated compared to medical sources (50.2%) (See Table 6.10).

* p1 = proportion for medical reporting sources, p2 = proportion for non-medical sources.

TABLE 6.10
REPORTING SOURCES BY DISPOSITIONS FOR PHYSICAL AND
SEXUAL CHILD ABUSE REPORTS

| | Dispositions n = 55 | | | |
Reporting Sources	% Substantiated	% Unsubstantiated	Total	n
Medical	49.8	50.2	38.9	217
Non-medical	33.7	66.3	61.1	341
Total	40.0	60.0	100.0	558

These findings reflect that reports from medical sources are more frequently substantiated, and reports from non-medical reporting sources are less frequently substantiated. And, the inverse relationship exists for reports that are unsubstantiated. Thus, the findings indicate that the dispositions of substantiated and unsubstantiated child abuse tend to be associated with a particular reporting source.

Because physical and sexual child abuse have different manifestations in terms of child maltreatment, the following sections examine the relationship between reporting sources and report dispositions according to the type of abuse.

Physical Abuse Reports

The analysis of physical abuse reports indicate that medical and non-medical reports are also statistically different (p<.05, p1 .435 - p2 .309 = .126, z = 2.37) in relationship to the report dispositions of substantiated and unsubstantiated. The findings for physical abuse reports represent approximately the same outcomes as reflected in the combined analysis of physical abuse reports. Specifically, physical abuse reports from medical sources (43.5%), as illustrated in Table 6.11, are substantiated more often for child abuse compared to physical abuse reports substantiated from non-medical sources (30.9%). Whereas physical abuse reports from non-medical sources (69.1%) are unsubstantiated more often compared to physical abuse reports from medical sources (56.5%). From these findings a significant difference (p.<.05) in reporting was found. The findings represent the predicated relationship for the study. It was predicted that reports from medical reporting sources would be substantiated more often than reports from non-medical reporting sources, and reports from non-medical reporting sources would be unsubstantiated more often than reports from medical reporting sources.

* p1 = proportion for medical reporting sources, p2 = proportion for non-medical reporting sources.

TABLE 6.11
REPORTING SOURCES BY DISPOSITIONS FOR PHYSICAL
CHILD ABUSE REPORTS

Reporting Sources	% Substantiated	% Unsubstantiated	Total	n
Medical	43.5	56.5	31.3	124
Non-Medical	30.9	69.1	68.7	272
Total	34.8	65.2	100.0	396

Dispositions n = 396

Sexual Abuse Reports

The analysis of sexual abuse reports indicate that medical and non-medical reporting sources are statistically different (p<.05, *p1 .581 - p2 .449 = .132, z = 1.67) in relationship to the report dispositions of substantiated and unsubstantiated child abuse. Sexual abuse reports from medical sources (58.1%) are more often substantiated for abuse than sexual abuse reports from non-medical sources (44.9%). Sexual abuse reports not substantiated for abuse are more often reported from non-medical sources (55.1%) compared to unsubstantiated sexual abuse reports from medical sources (41.9%) (See Table 6.12). These finding indicate a significant difference (p.<.05) in reporting and represented the predicted relationship. It was predicted that reports from medical reporting sources would be substantiated more often than reports from non-medical sources, and reports from non-medical sources would be unsubstantiated more often than reports from medical sources.

* p1 = proportion for medical reporting sources, p2 = proportion for non-medical reporting sources.

TABLE 6.12
REPORTING SOURCES BY DISPOSITIONS FOR SEXUAL
CHILD ABUSE REPORTS

Reporting Sources	Dispositions n = 162			
	% Substantiated	% Unsubstantiated	Total	n
Medical	58.1	41.9	57.4	93
Non-medical	44.9	55.1	42.6	69
Total	52.5	47.5	100.0	162

Overall, the analysis of physical and sexual abuse reports together and separately indicate that reports from medical and non-medical sources differ in terms of the type of dispositions more often rendered. Physical abuse reports and sexual abuse reports both indicated the same pattern of substantiation and unsubstantiation.

CONCLUSION

In summary, two critical findings have emerged from this study. First, the findings indicate that medical and non-medical reporting sources report different characteristics of children, families, and perpetrators as well as types and degree of severity in abuse. And secondly, the findings also indicate that report dispositions for alleged child abuse are related to the reporting sources. Specifically, the findings indicate reports generated from medical sources and non-medical sources in this study have different report disposition patterns (i.e., substantiated or unsubstantiated).

VII

DISCUSSION AND IMPLICATIONS

This final chapter discusses the study findings in relationship to previous research, and presents implications for future research and child welfare practices in child abuse.

DISCUSSION

The objective of the study presented is to determine whether certain report characteristics and dispositions of suspected child abuse incidents are related to a particular reporting source. This study examined the differences between suspected child abuse reports from medical and non-medical reporting sources in relationship to the characteristics of reported children, their families, the alleged perpetrators, and the report dispositions of substantiated and unsubstantiated child abuse. The data revealed that the report characteristics and dispositions are related to the reporting sources, confirming the hypotheses presented in this study.

Specifically, the data shows that medical sources, more often than non-medical sources, reported children with visible physical injuries, children who are young, black, and male, where the alleged abuse is perpetrated by "others" than mother or father, and from families residing in poverty areas. Reports from non-medical sources identified children with no visible physical injuries, older children, white and other race children, with mothers as the alleged perpetrators from families residing in non-poverty areas. Thus, the findings present that medical and non-medical sources differ significantly in the types of children and families reported in the incidents alleged. Confirming the second hypothesis, the data shows that reports from medical sources are more often substantiated than those from a non-medical source.

89

Conversely, reports from non-medical sources are more often unsubstantiated than those from medical sources.

The results of this study conform with previous research in relationship to the findings that the children most often reported by medical sources to have sustained visible injuries (external and internal injuries), are young, black, male, and whose families reside in poverty areas. The findings of this study depart, however, from previous research with respect to the characteristics of sexual abuse allegations, age of caretakers, and alleged perpetrators. From previous research it was reported that medical sources would report incidents of alleged sexual abuse and caretakers who are young more frequently than non-medical sources. However, this study found no significant difference between reports from medical and non-medical sources on these characteristics.

A third characteristic concerning the alleged perpetrator also differs from the literature. It was expected that mothers/mother substitutes would be the perpetrator category alleged most often by medical sources compared to non-medical sources. However, this study found medical reporters alleged "other" individuals (i.e., other female/male relatives, female/male non-relatives, school/professional child care providers, and non-professional baby-sitters) most often as perpetrators of physical child abuse compared to non-medical sources.

This finding is interesting because biological mothers are the largest group of alleged perpetrators in the study sample, while "other" individuals are the smallest group in the sample. Thus, medical sources reported the smallest group, "other" individuals most frequently.

As indicated earlier in Chapter 2 from the review of the literature, non-medical sources have been studied less frequently. However, this study's findings contrast with those of previous research on the characteristics of age of child, race of child, and type of injury. Previous research indicated that non-medical sources reported young and older children equally, black children, and children with visible injuries more often. This study found that older, white children with no visible injuries were reported most frequently by non-medical reporters compared to medical reporters. While provocative, the scant existing literature on non-medical reporters limits conjecture on these findings.

The findings regarding report dispositions are as predicted from previous research. Disposition is related to report source. The data in this study show that reports from medical sources are substantiated more often than reports from non-medical sources. Conversely, reports from non-medical reporting sources are unsubstantiated more often than reports from medical sources. The literature predicts this lack of substantiation unless the non-medical category is broken down into its component parts: law enforcement agencies, schools, etc. The literature shows that reports from law enforcement agencies are increasingly beginning to show a higher rate of substantiated over medical reports.

IMPLICATIONS

Future Research

From the ecological perspective guiding this study, further research is needed into the phenomenon of reporting. Three general directions of inquiry are suggested from the ecological perspective. What are the factors that influence potential reporters in their decision to report? What are the factors in the abusing incident that affect whether it will be reported? Do the attributes of the report source influence the investigation outcome?

These questions are suggested because the ecological perspective focuses our attention on the social and environmental influences on the individual reporter. These influences include: 1) maltreatment as an interactive event between the child and the perpetrator, 2) reporting as interactive and volitional, not automatic; and 3) the influence of reporters on the decision-making process of investigators of the reports.

This study, having demonstrated that report sources do differ in the types of children and incidents reported, suggests that it is important for the protection of children that further research be continued. Specific research is needed to address further what factors account for the decision to report, so that different types of children may be protected by various reporters. Some factors that are suggested as influential and need further study are:

- individual beliefs about what is maltreatment and what is the proper role of state intervention into the private family sphere;
- knowledge of the child protection system and the reporter's role in it;
- individual's confidence in the child protection system;

- the culture of the social system in which the potential reporter is embedded;
- professional background and training of the potential reporter;
- resources available to diagnose abuse; and
- stereotypes about who is likely to be an abuser and a victim of abuse.

The findings of this study suggest the behavior of the abuser is likely to bring attention to them. This is an area for further study. This study shows that low income families more often use hospitals/clinics, who report abuse at a substantially higher rate than private physicians, thus increasing their chances of being reported. Thus low income families suspected of child abuse may be more likely to be reported as a result of the type of health care facilities they use. Further investigation is essential into the critical question of whether the higher representation of blacks and low income persons is due to higher incidences of abuse within these groups or because of their coming to the attention of predisposed reporting sources.

The findings of this study regarding report substantiation supports the widely held belief that reports from medical sources are substantiated more often than those from non-medical sources. What is needed next is examination into this pattern that exists. It could be because medical reporters are better able to provide documentation (i.e., medical records, x-rays) of non-accidental injury leading to easier substantiation. However, another direction is also suggested. Are the investigating child protective services workers influenced by the prestige or non-prestige of a reporting source? Does a report from a valued institution (a hospital) by a respected reporter (a medical doctor) carry more influence with the investigator than a report by an anonymous or other non-professional source? The ecological perspective would suggest we should look to social/cultural factors in addition to documentation to examine the question why reports from some sources are substantiated at a greater rate than others.

Child Welfare Practice

Findings reported in this study on Urban Medical and Non-Medical Child Abuse Reporting recognized medical documentation as a key indicator of child abuse. These findings introduce a beginning foundation for practitioners involved in the investigation of child abuse to explore a multitude of factors within the environment that denote child maltreatment apart from the tangible evidence that some reporting sources most often give. Child welfare practitioners must continue to examine intensely the value of non-medical reporters in the child protection network. These reporters encounter populations of abused children that differ from those of medical reporters, and who often exhibit indicators of abuse that are much more difficult to fit into the concrete definitions for substantiating child abuse.

Furthermore, practitioners' insight into examining abuse as it is manifested within the culture and social systems of which the child is a member, is an ongoing process of critical importance. CPS practitioners must also realize the extent to which the social system of reporters is in constant flux. Therefore, these practitioners must heighten their professional awareness and sensitivity to the environmental dynamics of the systems generating reports, as well as to how the reported children and their families are embedded into the environment of the reporters. Consequently, it is particularly important that child protective services programs make available needed resources to facilitate practitioners to thoroughly assess the systemic dynamics impacting on reporters and reported children and their families; and the escalating number of alleged abuse reports received. Understanding the interactive process of abuse and reporting as it is impacted upon by our society will, indeed, enable child welfare practitioners to help prevent, identify, and provide interventive services in our communities to deal with the problem of child maltreatment (abuse).

CONCLUSION

Overall, this book has attempted to look at child abuse reporting from the aspects of medical and non-medical reporters. It is apparent that these two reporting sources report different segments of the population of children, families, and alleged perpetrators for child abuse. Furthermore, there is a recognizable difference in the substantiation and unsubstantiation rates of reports from these sources. Even more interesting, the book provides support for existing research pertaining to medical reporting and also presents relationships that are in contrast to the limited literature on non-medical reporting source. Essentially, using an ecological perspective of child abuse reporting, this book acknowledges the critical positions that various social systems at different levels (micro and macro) have on reporting and the investigation of abuse. And, finally for child protective services practitioners, it reports an additional framework for examining the reporting behavior of various reporters in the community child protection network, as well as a beginning for further research on child abuse reporting.

Appendix A

Maryland Child Abuse Reporting Laws and Statistics

MARYLAND CHILD ABUSE REPORTING LAW
DEFINITIONS OF DISPOSITIONS

Effective July 1, 1988

1. *Confirmed* means that there is credible and specific evidence that non-accidental injury or sexual abuse of a child occurred and was committed by a child's caretaker and this evidence has not been satisfactorily refuted. This determination does not depend upon a court conviction for the felony of child abuse or the existence of proof sufficient to obtain such a conviction.

2. *Indicated* means that there is a strong suspicion based on reasonable judgement that abuse occurred. Several indicative factors are usually found together when child abuse is likely in a situation of being investigated. These may include the nature, location, and extent of injuries that makes a non-accidental cause unlikely; a pattern of prior unexplained injuries in the family; evidence of sexual abuse; explanations that are inadequate, inconsistent, or that do not match the developmental age and capabilities of the child; and the credibility of the child's statement.

3. *Uncertain* means that it is not possible at the time when the investigation is completed to determine whether child abuse has occurred.

4. *Ruled Out* means that there was no injury or acts of abuse perpetrated against the child, or that injuries clearly have been accidentally caused, or there was injury or sexual abuse of the child but it was know to have been committed by someone, such as a neighbor or stranger or any other identified person, who did not have care or custody of the child (Subtitle 7, Regulations 07.02.07.07 Maryland Family Law Code Annotated July 1988).

MARYLAND CHILD ABUSE REPORTING LAW
DEFINITIONS OF DISPOSITIONS

Effective October 1, 1994

1. *Indicated* means a finding that there is credible evidence, which has not been satisfactorily refuted, that abuse, neglect, or sexual abuse did occur.

2. *Ruled out* means a finding that abuse, neglect, or sexual abuse did not occur.

3. *Unsubstantiated* means a finding that there is an insufficient amount of evidence to support a finding of indicated or ruled out (Subtitle 7, 5-701 Maryland's Civil Child Abuse and Neglect Law October 1994)

Figure A.1

Maryland Investigations for FY 1994

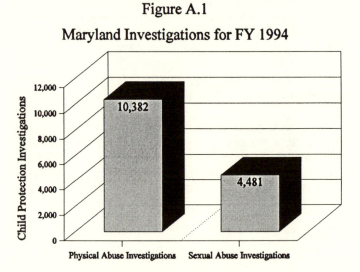

Source: Maryland Dept. of Human Services, 1995

Appendix B

Codebook and Schedule for Urban Medical and Non-Medical Reports

CODEBOOK FOR STUDY ON URBAN MEDICAL
AND NON-MEDICAL ABUSE REPORTS

The codebook provides instruction for collecting data relevant to the study variables (measures). Coded data is recorded on the coding schedule as indicated in the explanation of each variable. The number and variable titles on the coding schedule correspond to the number and title of variables described in this codebook.

V 1. Report Identification Number: To ensure that a report is correctly identified use the 3 digit number located at the top of the report. This variable is coded according to the following instruction:

      3 digits coded 00X - XXX (e.g. 001 - 123)

Use columns 1 thru 3 of the coding schedule.

V 2. Census Tract: The information is the census tract that tells where the child's caretaker lived at the time of the alleged abusive incident. The information is the 5 digit number found at the top of the report. Use column 4 thru 9 of the coding schedule.

V 3. Number of Child Victims Reported: This variable identifies how many children are alleged by the reporter to have been abused. The information is found on the intake sheet and/or narrative summary section of the report. Verify information by checking both sections of the report. Use columns 10 thru 11 of the coding schedule.

V 4. Source of Report: This variable identifies the source of the child abuse report. Information pertaining to the reporting source can be found at the top of the report or in the narrative summary. Reporting sources are categorized as Medical=1 or Non-Medical=2. Use column 12 of the coding schedule.

Medical Report Sources: Medical facility personnel are professionals working in a health care facility including the physician, nurse, social worker, therapist, technician, etc. A health care facility includes acute, chronic, and mental hospitals as well as their out-patient clinics, health department clinics, family planning clinics, and well-baby clinics. They include:

     a. Johns Hopkins Hospital
     b. University Hospital
     c. Sinai Hospital
     d. Mercy Hospital
     e. Union Memorial
     f. Wyman Park
     g. North Charles General Hospital
     h. Baltimore City Hospitals
     i. Maryland General Hospital
     j. South Baltimore General
     k. Bon Secours Hospital
     l. Good Samaritan Hospital
     m. Lutheran Hospital

Private practitioners include medical doctors, social workers, psychologists, technicians, etc. who discovers maltreatment during the course of seeing a private practice client.

Non-Medical Report Sources: Any persons employed in a public or private social services agency, child care facility, day care center, public or private school, law enforcement and judicial system, and recreational center; parents, relatives, neighbors, friends, victims, etc.; and anonymous.

V 5. Physical Abuse Allegation: This variable identifies the stated alleged physical abuse of the child(ren) in the report. Information is located in the narrative summary section of the report. The variable is coded according to the following classifications:

     0=No visible injury includes reports stating the child was beaten, punched, slapped, or bitten even though no injury is evident.
     1=Visible injury includes reports stating the child had bruises, cuts, abrasions, burns, contusions, fractures, internal injuries, was poisoned, or died.

Use column 13 of the coding schedule.

V 6. Sexual Abuse Allegation: This variable identifies the stated alleged sexual abuse of the child(ren) in the report. Information is located in the narrative summary section of the report. The variable is coded according to the following classifications:

> 0=No specific sexual act includes reports that implies the child had a venereal disease, sexual tickling, child is encouraged, pressured, or propositioned to perform sexual acts (but no sexual activity or molestation occurred), and sexual exhibitionism.
>
> 1=Specific sexual act includes reports that one or more of the following acts took place, such as touching/fondling of genitals or breast (maybe mutual, digital intercourse, oral intercourse, fellation or cunnilingus, anal intercourse, and genital intercourse).

Use column 14 of the coding schedule.

V 7. Age of the Reported Child(ren): This variable identifies the age of the child(ren) at the time of the report. This information was obtained by using the month and year of birth on the report for the child(ren). The variable is coded as follows:

> 0=Young children-infancy to 9 years.
> 1=Older children-ages 10 to 17 years.

Use column 15 of the coding schedule.

V 8. Race of reported child(ren): This variable identifies the race of the child(ren) as indicated on the report. The variable is coded as follows:

> 0=Black
> 1=White
> 2=Others (i.e. Hispanics, Native Americans, Asian/Pacific Islanders, bi-racial, and other racial groups not recognized as blacks or whites.

Use column 16 of the coding schedule.

V 9. Sex of reported child(ren): This variable identifies the sex recorded for the child on the report. The variable is coded as follows:

> 0=Male
> 1=Female

Use column 17 of the coding schedule.

V10. Age of permanent caretaker(s): This variable allows for the identification of the age of the child's caretaker(s) at the time of the report. Two caretakers maybe recorded if indicated in the report. Record the first caretaker according to the individual who has primary responsibility for the permanent care of the child(ren). The variable is coded as follows:

> 0=Young caretakers are ages 15 to 24 years.
> 1=Older caretakers are ages 25 years and older.

Use column 18 of the coding schedule for the first caretaker's age and column 19 for the second caretaker's age.

V11. Alleged perpetrator(s): This variable identifies the alleged perpetrator's relationship to the child(ren). If reported two perpetrators may be indicated. Use the information located in the narrative summary section. The information is coded as follows:

> 0=Mothers/mother substitutes (biological mothers, foster mothers, stepmothers, and father's paramour)
> 1=Father/father substitutes (biological fathers, foster fathers, stepfathers, and mother's paramour)
> 2=Other individuals (other female/male relatives, female/male non-relatives, school or professional child care providers, and non-professional baby-sitters)

Use column 20 if there is only one perpetrator and column 21 for a second perpetrator on the coding schedule.

V12. Socio-economic status (ses) of families area of residence: This variable determines whether the reported families lived in a poverty or non poverty area of the city. The variable is coded as follows:

> 0=Non-poverty area
> 1=Poverty area

Use column 22 of the coding schedule.

V13. Disposition: This variable identifies the disposition given to reports after the investigation. The variable was collapsed into two categories and coded as follows:

> 0=Unsubstantiated (uncertain and rules out)
> 1=Substantiated (confirmed and indicated)

Use column 23 of the coding schedule.

These coding categories are based on Subtitle 7, Regulations 07.02.07.07 of the Maryland Family Law Code Annotated July 1, 1988.

URBAN MEDICAL AND NON-MEDICAL REPORTS
CODING SCHEDULE

Coding Notes: 8 or 98 = missing data
                   9 or 99 = not applicable

1. Report identification number...(3 digits coded 00X - XXX)

$$\overline{1}\ \overline{2}\ \overline{3}$$

2. Census Tract ... (3 digits coded 0XXX00, 4 digits XXXX000)

$$\overline{4}\ \overline{5}\ \overline{6}\ \overline{7}\ \overline{8}\ \overline{9}$$

3. Number of child victims reported.

$$\overline{10}\ \overline{11}$$

4. Source of Report ... (1=medical, 2=non-medical)

$$\overline{12}$$

5. Physical Abuse Allegation......(0=no visible injury,
   1=visible injury)

$$\overline{13}$$

6. Sexual Abuse Allegation..(0=no specific sexual act,
   1=specific sexual act)

$$\overline{14}$$

7. Age of reported child ...(0=young children - 9 years to
   infancy, 1=older children - 10 years to 17 years)

$$\overline{15}$$

8. Race of reported children..(0=black, 1=white, 2=others)

$$\overline{16}$$

9. Sex of reported children...(0=male, 1=female)

$$\overline{17}$$

10. Age of permanent caretaker ...(0=young caretakers - 24 years and younger, 1=older caretakers - 25 years and older)

$\overline{\quad\quad}$
18

$\overline{\quad\quad}$
19

11. Alleged perpetrators...(0=mothers/mother substitutes, 1=fathers/father substitutes, 2=other individuals)

$\overline{\quad\quad}$
20

$\overline{\quad\quad}$
21

12. Socioeconomic status of reported family residence ... (0=non-poverty areas, 2=poverty areas)

$\overline{\quad\quad}$
22

13. Disposition . . . (0=unsubstantiated, 1=substantiated)

$\overline{\quad\quad}$
23

ITEMS 5 THROUGH 12 REPEAT FOR REMAINING REPORTED CHILDREN

Appendix C

Urban Medical and Non-Medical Reporting Figures

Analysis of Urban Medical and Non-Medical Reports
Allegations of Physical Abuse

Figure C.1a

No Visible Physical Injury

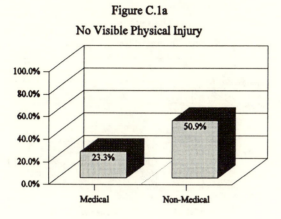

Figure C.1b

Visible Physical Injury

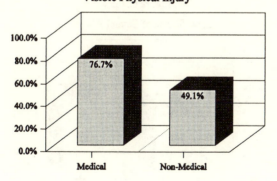

Analysis of Urban Medical and Non-Medical Reports
Allegations of Sexual Abuse

Figure C.2a

No Specific Act of Sexual Abuse

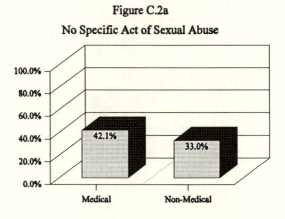

Figure C.2b

Specific Act of Sexual Abuse

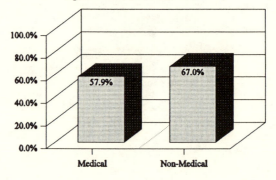

Analysis of Urban Medical Reports
Age of Reported Children by Type of Abuse

Figure C.3a

Physical and Sexual Abuse Reports

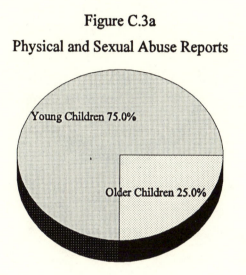

Young children - infants to 9 years
Older children - 10 to 17 years

Analysis of Urban Medical Reports
Age of Reported Children by Type of Abuse

Figure C.3b
Physical Abuse Reports

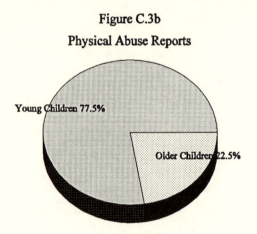

Young Children 77.5%

Older Children 22.5%

Figure C.3c
Sexual Abuse Reports

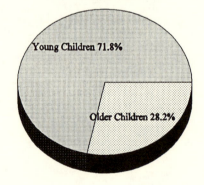

Young Children 71.8%

Older Children 28.2%

Analysis of Urban Medical Reports
Race of Reported Children by Type of Abuse

Figure C.4a

Physical and Sexual Abuse Reports

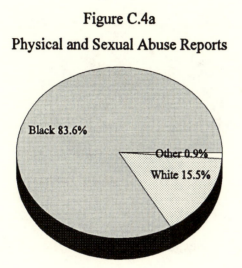

Analysis of Urban Medical Reports
Race of Reported Children by Type of Abuse

Figure C.4b

Physical Abuse Reports

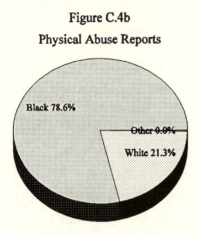

Figure C.4c

Sexual Abuse Reports

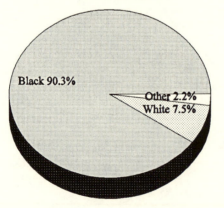

Analysis of Urban Medical Reports
Sex of Reported Children by Type of Abuse

Figure C.5a

Physical and Sexual Abuse Reports

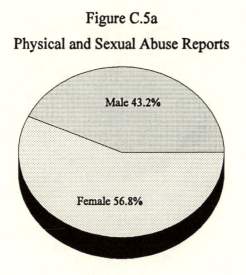

Analysis of Urban Medical Reports
Sex of Reported Children by Type of Abuse

Figure C.5b
Physical Abuse Reports

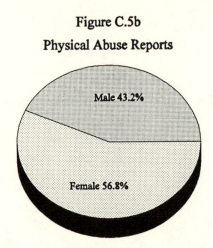

Male 43.2%

Female 56.8%

Figure C.5c
Sexual Abuse Reports

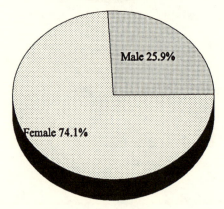

Male 25.9%

Female 74.1%

Analysis of Urban Non-Medical Report
Age of Reported Children by Type of Abuse

Figure C.6a

Physical and Sexual Abuse Reports

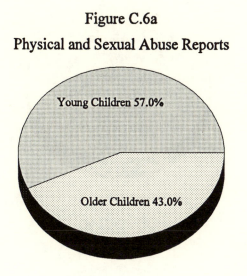

Young children - infants to 9 years
Older children - 10 to 17 years

Analysis of Urban Non-Medical Reports
Age of Reported Children by Type of Abuse

Figure C.6b
Physical Abuse Reports

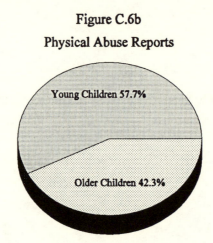

Figure C.6c
Sexual Abuse Reports

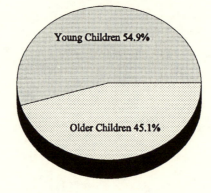

Analysis of Urban Non-Medical Reports
Race of Reported Children by Type of Abuse

Figure C.7a

Physical and Sexual Abuse Reports

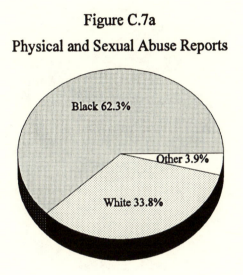

Analysis of Urban Non-Medical Reports
Race of Reported Children by Type of Abuse

Figure C.7b

Physical Abuse Reports

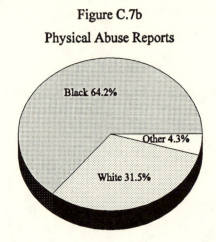

Figure C.7c

Sexual Abuse Reports

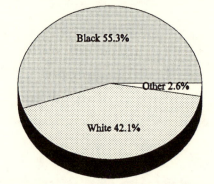

Analysis of Urban Non-Medical Reports
Sex of Reported Children by Type of Abuse

Figure C.8a

Physical and Sexual Abuse Reports

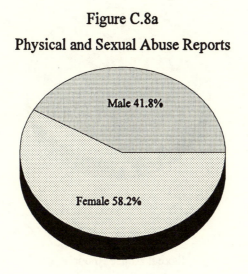

Analysis of Urban Non-Medical Report
Sex of Reported Children by Type of Abuse

Figure C.8b
Physical Abuse Reports

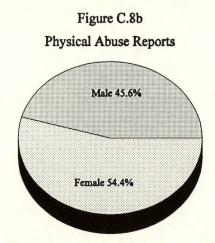

Figure C.8c
Sexual Abuse Reports

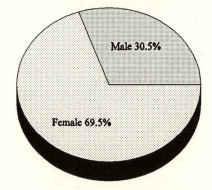

Analysis of Urban Medical Repor s
Age of Reported Caretakers by Type of Abuse

Figure C.9a

Physical and Sexual Abuse Reports

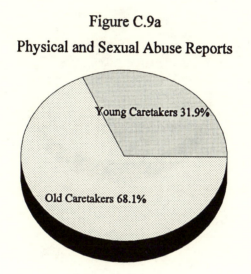

Young Caretakers - 15 to 24 years
Old Caretakers - 25 years and older

Analysis of Urban Medical Report
Age of Reported Caretakers by Type of Abuse

Figure C.9b
Physical Abuse Reports

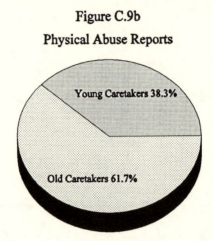

Young Caretakers 38.3%

Old Caretakers 61.7%

Figure C.9c
Sexual Abuse Reports

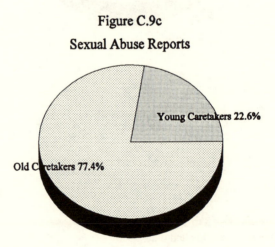

Young Caretakers 22.6%

Old Caretakers 77.4%

Analysis of Urban Non-Medical Reports
Age of Reported Caretakers by Type of Abuse

Figure C.10a

Physical and Sexual Abuse Reports

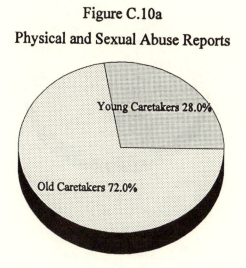

Young Caretakers - 15 to 24 years
Old Caretakers - 25 years and older

Analysis of Urban Non-Medical Report
Age of Reported Caretakers by Type of Abuse

Figure C.10b
Physical Abuse Reports

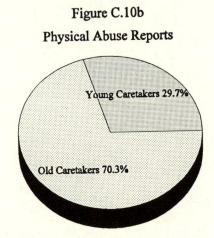

Figure C.10c
Sexual Abuse Reports

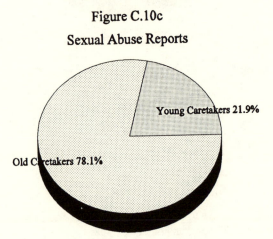

Analysis of Urban Medical Reports
Alleged Perpetrators by Type of Abuse

Figure C.11a

Physical and Sexual Abuse Reports

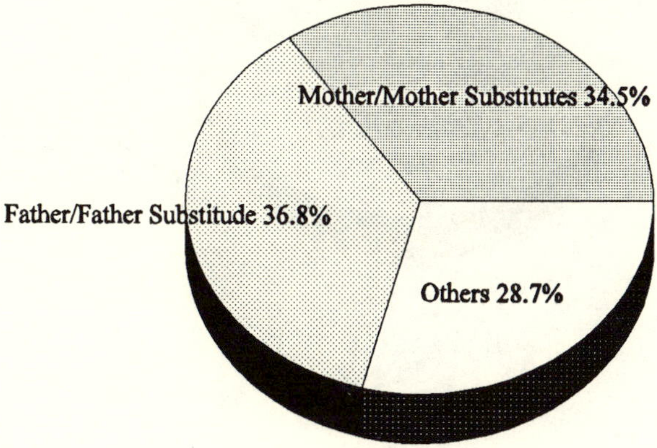

Mother/Mother Substitutes 34.5%

Father/Father Substitude 36.8%

Others 28.7%

Analysis of Urban Medical Report
Alleged Perpetrators by Type of Abuse

Figure C.11b
Physical Abuse Reports

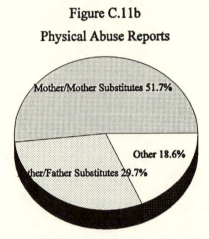

Mother/Mother Substitutes 51.7%

Other 18.6%

...her/Father Substitutes 29.7%

Figure C.11c
Sexual Abuse Reports

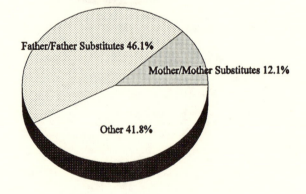

Father/Father Substitutes 46.1%

Mother/Mother Substitutes 12.1%

Other 41.8%

Analysis of Urban Non-Medical Reports
Alleged Perpetrator by Type of Abuse

Figure C.12a

Physical and Sexual Abuse Reports

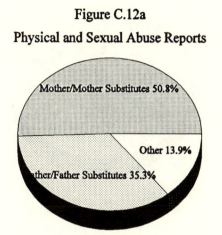

Mother/Mother Substitutes 50.8%

Other 13.9%

ther/Father Substitutes 35.3%

Analysis of Urban Non-Medical Report
Alleged Perpetrators by Type of Abuse

Figure C.12b
Physical Abuse Reports

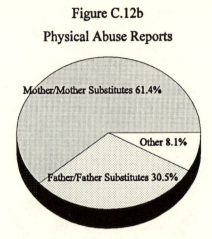

Figure C.12c
Sexual Abuse Reports

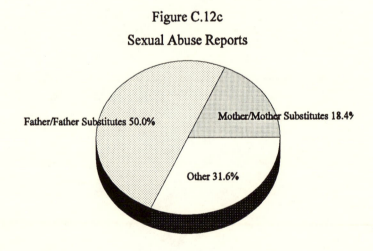

Analysis of Urban Medical Reports
Reported Family Areas of Residence by Type of Abuse

Figure C.13a

Physical and Sexual Abuse Reports

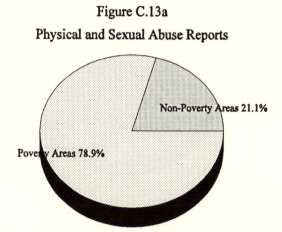

Non-Poverty Areas 21.1%

Poverty Areas 78.9%

Analysis of Urban Medical Report
Reported Family Areas of Residence by Type of Abuse

Figure C.13b
Physical Abuse Reports

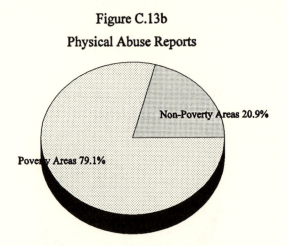

Non-Poverty Areas 20.9%

Poverty Areas 79.1%

Figure C.13c
Sexual Abuse Reports

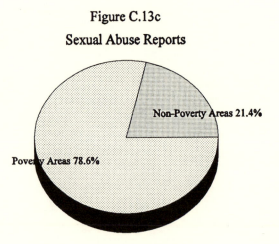

Non-Poverty Areas 21.4%

Poverty Areas 78.6%

Analysis of Urban Non-Medical Reports
Reported Family Areas of Residence by Type of Abuse

Figure C.14a

Physical and Sexual Abuse Reports

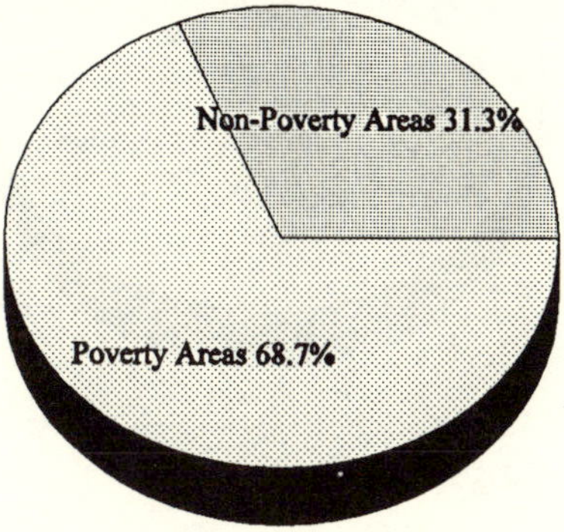

Non-Poverty Areas 31.3%

Poverty Areas 68.7%

Analysis of Urban Non-Medical Report
Reported Family Areas of Residence by Type of Abuse

Figure C.14b
Physical Abuse Reports

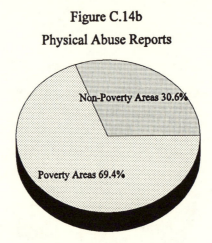

Non-Poverty Areas 30.6%

Poverty Areas 69.4%

Figure C.14c
Sexual Abuse Reports

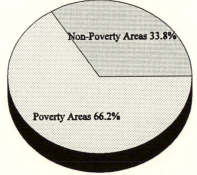

Non-Poverty Areas 33.8%

Poverty Areas 66.2%

Urban Medical and Non-Medical Report
Substantiation Rates

Figure C.15a

Physical and Sexual Abuse Reports

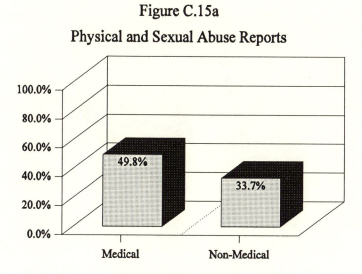

Urban Medical and Non-Medical Report
Substantiation Rates

Figure C.15b
Physical Abuse Reports

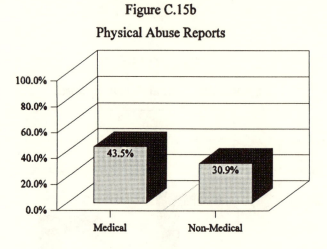

Figure C.15c
Sexual Abuse Reports

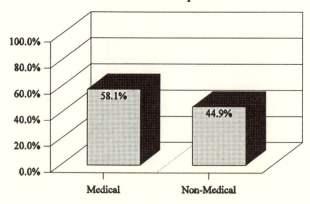

Urban Medical and Non-Medical Report
Unsubstantiation Rates

Figure C.16a

Physical and Sexual Abuse Reports

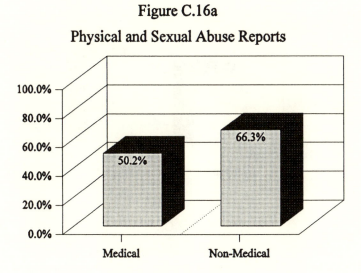

Urban Medical and Non-Medical Report Unsubstantiation Rates

Figure C.16b
Physical Abuse Reports

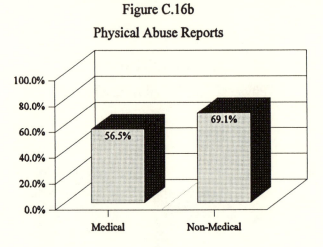

Figure C.16c
Sexual Abuse Reports

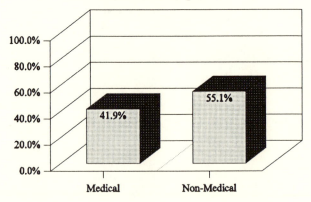

Appendix D

Study Site Map

Baltimore City, MD
Census Tracts

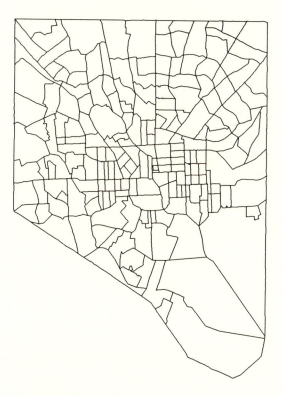

Source: 1990 U.S. Bureau of the Census

References

Abramczyk, Lois W. and Sweigart, Cindy. 1985. *Child abuse and neglect: Indicate vs unfounded report characteristics.* South Carolina: College of Social Work, University of South Carolina.

Adamowicz, D. 1976. "Child abuse and neglect: The problem and its management," *DHEW Publications.* nos: 75-30073, 75-30074, & 75-30075: 1-63, 1-89, & 1-208.

Adams, W., Barone, N., and Tooman, P. "The dilemma of anonymous reporting in child protective services." *Child Welfare* 6(1) (January): 3-14.

Altemeier, W.A., S. O'Connor, P. Vietze, H. Sandler and K. Sherrod. 1984 "Prediction of child abuse: A prospective study of feasibility," *Child Abuse and Neglect.* 8: 393-400.

Alter, Catherine Foster. 1985a. "Interorganizational service delivery Systems: A process model." Doctoral Dissertation, University of Maryland School of Social Work and Community Planning.

_____. 1985b. "Decision-making factors in cases of child neglect." *Child Welfare.* 64(2) (March-April): 99-111.

Alvy, K.1975. "Preventing child abuse." *American Psychologist.* 30: 921-928.

American Humane Association. 1987. *National analysis of official child neglect and abuse reporting.* Denver: American Humane Association.

American Humane Association. 1985. *National analysis of official child neglect and abuse reporting.* Denver: American Humane Association.

American Humane Association. 1978. *National analysis of official child neglect and abuse reporting.* Denver: American Humane Association.

Antler, S. 1978. "Child abuse: An emerging social priority." *Social Work.* 23(1):58-61.

Bailey, Kenneth D. 1978. *Methods of social research*. New York: The Free Press.

Baldwin, J. A. and Oliver, J. E. 1975. "Epidemiology and family characteristics of severely abused children." *British Journal of Preventive Social Medicine*. 29: 205-11.

Barth, R., Berrick, J. D., and Gilbert, N. 1994. *Child welfare research review: Volumn one*. New York: Columbia University Press.

Barth, R. P. 1985. "Collaboration between child welfare and school social work services." *Social Work in Education*. 8(1): 32-47.

Becker, H. 1963. *Outsiders: Studies in the sociology of deviance*. New York: Free Press.

_____. 1964. Perspectives on deviance: The other side. New York: Free Press.

Belsky, Jay. 1980. "Child maltreatment: An ecological integration." *American Psychologist*. 35(4) (April): 320-335.

_____. 1978a. "A theoretical analysis of child abuse remediation strategies." *Journal of Clinical Child Psychology*. 7:113-117.

_____. 1978b. "Three theoretical models of child abuse: A critical review. *International Journal of Child Abuse and Neglect*. 3:37-49.

ten Bensel, R.W. and Berdie J. 1976. "The neglect and abuse of children and youth: The scope of the problem and the school's role." *Journal of School Health*. 46(10): 453-61.

Bernstein, Arthur H. 1984. "Child abuse reports: Breach of medical confidentiality?" *Hospitals*. 58:13 (July): 86-88.

Besharov, Douglas J. 1983. "Protecting abused and neglected children: Can law help social work?" *Child Abuse and Neglect*. 7(4): 421-34.

_____.1985. "Right versus rights: The dilemma of child protection." *Public Welfare*. 43(2): 19-27.

_____. 1984. "Liability in child welfare." *Public Welfare*. 42 (Spring): 28-33.

_____. 1986. "Unfounded allegations: A new child abuse problem," the public interest. 83 (Spring): 18-33.

_____. 1987. "Reporting out-of-home maltreatment penalties and protections." *Child Welfare*. 66: 399-408.

_____. 1990. *Recognizing child abuse: A guide for the conerned*. New York: The Free Press.

Biddle, Bruce. 1979. Rôle theory expectation, identities, and behavior. New York: Academic Press.

Billingsley, Andrew. 1964. "The role of the social worker in a child protective agency" *Child Welfare.* 43 (October): 472-480.

Billingsley, A., and Giovannoni, J. M. 1972. Children of the storm: Black children and American child welfare. New York: Harcourt, Brace, Jovanovich, Inc.

Blalock, Hubert M. 1979. *Social statistics.* 2nd edition. New York: McGraw Hill Book Company.

Blau, Peter M. 1974. On the nature of organization. New York: John Wiley & Sons.

Blum, R. W. and Runyan, C. 1980. "Adolescent abuse: The dimensions of the problem." *Journal of Adolescent Health Care.* 1(2) (December): 121-6.

Blumberg, M. L. 1974. "Psychopathology of the abusing parent," *American Journal of Psychotherapy.* 28: 21.

Boje, David M. and Whetten, David A. 1981. "Effects of organizational strategies and contextual constraints on centrality and attributions of interorganizational networks." *Administrative Science Quarterly.* 26(3): 378-95.

Brannon, D. 1985. "Decision-making in public welfare: Scientific management meets organized anarchy." *Administration in Social Work.* 9(1): 23-33.

Bronfenbrenner, U. 1979. *The ecology of human development.* Cambridge, Mass.: Harvard University Press.

Burnley, Jane N. 1986. "Child protection's future is under debate." *National Association of Social Work News.* 3(4) (April): 5.

Butz, Randall A. 1985. "Reporting child abuse and confidentiality in counseling." *Social Casework.* 66(2): 83-90.

Caffey, J. 1946. "Multiple fractures in the long bones of infants suffering from chronic subdural hematoma." *American Journal of Roentgenol.* 56 (August): 163-173.

Cain, L. P. 1980. "Child abuse: Historical precedent and legal ramifications." *Health and Social Work.* 5(3) (August): 61-67.

Children's Defense Fund. 1989. *A vision for America's future - agenda for the 1990s: A children's defense budget.* Washington, D.C.

Colucci, N. D. 1977. "The schools and the problem of child abuse and neglect." *Contemporary Education.* XLVII.

Conrad, Peter and Schneider, Joseph W. 1989. "Looking at levels of medicalization: A comment on Strong's critique of the thesis of medical imperialism." *Social Science and Medicine.* 14A: 75-79.

Cook, Joanne Valianat and Bowles, Roy Tyler. 1980. *Child abuse: Commission and omission.* Toronto, Canada: Butterworth.

Council of Scientific Affairs. 1985. *"American Medical Association diagnostic and treatment guidelines concerning child abuse and neglect."* Journal of American Medical Association. 254(6) (August): 796-800.

Craft, John L. and Clarkson, Cheryl D. 1985. "Case disposition recommendation of attorneys and social workers in child abuse investigation." *Child Abuse and Neglect.* 9(2): 165-174

Craft, John L., Epley, Stephen, W., and Clarkson, Cheryl D. 1980. "Factors influencing legal dispositions in child abuse investigation." *Journal of Social Service Research.* 5: 61-81.

Crittenden, Patricia M. 1992. "The social ecology of treatment: Case study of a service systems for maltreatment children." *American Journal Orthopsychiatric.* 62(1) (January): 22-34.

Daley, Michael, and Piliavin, Irving. 1982. "Violence against children revisited: Some necessary clarification of findings from a major national study." *Journal of Social Service Research.* 5: 61-81.

Daniel, Jessica H., Hampton, Robert L., and Newberger, Eli N. (1987). "Child abuse and accidents in Black families: A controlled comparative study." In *Violence in Black families: Correlates and consequences.* 1st edition. ed. R. Hampton, 55-65. Massachusetts: Lexington Books.

Daniel, Jessica H., Hampton, Robert L. and Newberger, Eli H. "Child abuse and accidents in Black families: A controlled comparative Study." *American Journal of Orthopsychriatry.* 53(4) (October): 645-53.

Delvin, Mary M. 1983. "Reporting suspected child abuse." *Journal of the American Medical Association.* 249(15): 2017-18.

DiLeonardi, Joan W. 1980. "Decision making in protective services." *Child Welfare.* 59(9): 356-364.

Ditson, Joan and Shay, Sharon. 1984. "Use of a home-based microcomputer to analyze community data from reported cases of child abuse and neglect." *Child Abuse and Neglect.* 8: 503-509.

Doek, Jaap. 1984. "Policy options on child abuse and neglect." *Child Abuse and Neglect.* 8(4): 385-386.

Drews, Kay. 1980. "The role conflict of the child protective services worker: Investigator-helper." *Child Abuse and Neglect.* 4: 247-254.

Ebbin, A. J., Gollub, M. H., A. M. Stein and M. G. Wilson. 1969. "Battered child syndrome at Los Angeles County General Hospital." *American Journal of the Disease of Children.* 118: 660-67

England, B. and Brunnquell, B. A. 1979. "An at-risk approach to the study of child abuse." *Journal of American Academy of Child Pyschology.* 18: 219-35.

Elmer, E. 1977. "A follow-up study of traumatized children." *Pediatrics.* 59: 273-9.

Erickson, K. 1962. "Notes on the sociology of deviance." *Social Problems.* 9 (Spring): 307-14.

Faller, Kathleen C. 1981. *Social work with abused and neglected children: A manual of interdisciplinary practice.* New York: The Free Press.

_____. "Unanticipated problems in the United States child protection system." *Child Abuse and Neglect.* 9(2): 63-69.

Farber, Edward D. and Joseph, Jack A. 1985. "The maltreated adolescent: Patterns of physical abuse." *Child Abuse and Neglect.* 9: 201-206.

Fein, L. G. 1979. "Can child fatalities as end products of child abuse be prevented?" *Children and Youth Services Review.* 1(1): 31-53.

Finkelhor, David. 1984. *Child sexual abuse: New theory and research.* New York: The Free Press.

_____. 1983. "Removing the child-prosecuting the offender in cases of sexual abuse: Evidence from the national reporting system for child abuse and neglect." *Child Abuse and Neglect.* 7(2): 195-205.

_____. 1980. "Risk factors in the sexual victimization of children." *Child Abuse and Neglect.* 4: 265-273.

Fisher, B., Berdie, J., Cook, J., and Noel, D. 1980. "Adolescent abuse and neglect: Intervention strategies." *U. S. Department of Health and Human Services.* DHHS No. 80 (OHDS) (January): 230-266.

Flammang, C. A. 1984. *The police and the underprotected child.* Springfield Illinois: Charles C. Thomas.

Fontana, Vincent J. 1973. "The diagnosis of the maltreatment syndrome in children." *Pediatrics.* 51: 780-82.

Fontana, Vincent and Besharov, Douglas. 1977. *The maltreated child.* 3rd edition. Illinois: Charles C. Thomas Publisher.

Forcese, Dennis P. and Richer, Stephen. 1973. *Social research methods.* New Jersey: Prentice Hall, Inc.

Fraley, Yvonne L. 1969. "A role model for practice." *Social Service Review.* 43: 145-154.

Frischmeyer, Linda E. and Ballard, Dennis D. 1980. "Iowa professionals and the child abuse reporting statutes: A case of success." *Iowa Law Review.* 65 (July): 1273-1385.

Gaines, R., A. Sandgrund, A. H. Green and E. Bower. 1978. "Etiological factors in child maltreatment: A multivariate study of abusing, neglecting, and normal mothers." *Journal of Abnormal psychology.* 87: 531-401.

Garbarino, James. 1980. *Protecting children from abuse and neglect.* San Fransisco: Josey-Bass.

_____. 1979. "An ecological approach to child maltreatment." In *The social context of child abuse and neglect*, ed. L. Pelton, 228-267. New York: Human Sciences Press.

_____. 1977. "The human ecology of child matreatment: A conceptual model for research." *Journal of Marriage and the Family.* 39: 721-736.

Garbarino, James andf Ebata, Aaron. 1987. "The significance of ethnic and cultural differences in child maltreatment." In *Violence in Black families: Correlates and consequences,* 1st edition. ed. R. Hampton, 21-38. Massachusetts: Lexington Books.

Geiser, R. 1979. *Hidden victims: The sexual abuse of children.* Boston: Becon.

Gelles, Richard J. 1975. "The social construction of child abuse." *American Journal of Orthopsychiatry.* 44: 363-371.

Gelles, Richard J. and Lancaster, Jane B. 1987. *Child abuse and neglect: Biosocial dimensions.* New York: Aldine DeGruyter.

Gerbner, George, Ross, Catherine, and Zigler, Edward. 1980. *Child abuse : An agenda for action.* New York: Oxford University Press.

Ginsberg, Leon. 1995. *Social work almanac.* 2nd edition. Washington, DC: NASW Press.

Gil, David G. 1971. "Sociocultural perspective on physical child abuse." *Child Welfare.* vol. 1, no. 7 (July): 389-95.

_____. 1979. *Child abuse and violence.* New York: AMS Press, Inc.

_____. 1969. "Physical abuse of children: Findings and implications of a nationwide survey." *Pedicatrics.* 44: 857-64.

_____. 1979. "Unraveling child abuse." *American Journal of Orthopsychiatry.* 45: 325-55.

_____. 1970. *Violence against children: Physical child abuse in the United States.* Cambridge, Massachusetts: Harvard University Press.

_____. 1968. "Incidence of child abuse and demographic characteristics of persons involved." In *The battered child,* eds. R. E. Helfer and C. Henry Kempe, 19-40. Chicago: The University of Chicago Press.

Giovannoni, Jeanne M. 1980. "Unanswered cries: The problem of unsubstantiated child abuse." *Social Welfare.* 13-15.

Giovannoni, Jeanne M. and Becerra, Rosina M. 1979. *Defining child abuse.* New York: The Free Press.

Giovannoni, Jeanne M., Conklin, Jonathan, and Iiyama, Patti. 1978. *Child abuse and neglect: An examination for the perspective of child development knowledge.* California: R & E Research Associate, Inc.

Glaser, Danya, and Frosh, Stephen. 1988. *Child Sexual Abuse.* Illinois: The Dorsey Press.

Gleeson, Janmes P. 1984. *The use of structured decision-making procedures at child welfare intake.* Doctoral Dissertation, University of Chicago.

Governor's Task Force on Child Abuse and Neglect Final Report. 1985. Anapolis, Maryland.

Groenevld, Lyle P. and Giovannoni, Jeanne M. 1977. "Disposition of child abuse and neglect cases." *Social Work Research and Abrstracts.*13(2): 24-30.

Guyer, M. J. 1982. "Child abuse and neglect statutes: Legal and clinical implications." American Journal of Orthopsychiatry. 52(1): 73-81.

Hage, Jeral. 1980. *Theories of organizations form, process, and transformation.* New York: John Wiley & Son.

Hampton, Robert and Newberger, Eli H. 1985. "Child abuse incidence and reporting by hospital: Significance of severity, class, and race." *American Journal of Public Health*. 75(1): 56-60.

Hampton, Robert L. 1987a. "Violence against Black children: Current knowledge and future research needs." In *Violence in Black families: Correlates and consequences*, 1st edition. ed. R. Hampton, 4-20. Massachusetts: Lexington Books.

Hampton, Robert L. 1987b. "Race, class, and child maltreatment." *Journal of Comparative Family Studies*. 13(1): 113-126.

Hampton, Robert L. 1991. *Black family violence: Current research and theory*. Massachusetts: Lexington Books.

Hardy, Margaret E. and Conway, Mary E. 1978. *Role theory perspectives for health professionals*. New York: Appleton Century-Crofts, Prentice Hall, Inc.

Helfer, Ray E., and Kempe, Ruth S. 1987. *The battered child*. 4th edition. Chicago: The University of Chicago Press.

Herman, J. and Hirschman, L. 1977. "Father-daughter incest." *Signs*. 2: 735-756.

Holder, Wayne M. and Mohr, Cynthia. 1980. *Helping in child protective services*. Colorado: The American Humane Association.

Holter, J. and Friedman, S. 1968. "Child abuse: Early case findings in the emergency department." *Pediatrics*. 42: 128-38.

Holtzman, W. H. 1975. *Personality development in two cultures*. Texas: University of Texas Press.

Howing, Phyllis, John S. Wodarski, P. David Kurtz and James Martin Gaudin. 1993. *Maltreatment and the school-age child: Developmental outcomes and system issues*. New York: The Haworth Press, Inc.

Hurt, Mauree Jr. 1975. "Reporting, recording, and diagnosis." *Child Abuse and Neglect: A report on the status of the research*. DHEW Publication (OHD). Washington, DC, U.S. Department of Health, Education, and Welfare, 12-16.

Hyman, H. H. 1972, *Secondary analysis of sample survey: Principles, procedures, and potentialities*. New York: John Wiley and Sons, Inc.

Ivancevich, J. M. and Donnelly, J. H. 1974. "A study of role clarity and need for clarity for three occupational groups." *Academy of Management Journal.* 17(1): 28-38.

Jackson, A. 1983. "Professional and non-professional sources of child maltreatment reports." *For Your Information.* 4: 3-7.

Karger, Howard J. and Stoesz, David. 1994. *American social welfare policy: A pluralist approach.* 2nd edition. New York: Longman.

Kempe, C. Henry. 1962. "The battered child syndrome." *Journal of the American Medical Association.* 181: 105-112.

Kerns, David L. 1979. "Child abuse and neglect: Physicians role in diagnosis and reporting." *Connecticut Medicine.* 43(2): 89-92.

Kitsuse, J. 1964. "Societal reactions to deviant behavior: Problems of theory and methods." In Perspectives on deviance: The other side, ed. H. Becker, New York: Free Press.

Koerin, Beverly. 1980. "Child abuse and neglect: Changing policies and perspectives." *Child Welfare.* 59(9): 542-50.

Kotch, Jonathan B. and Thomas, L. Park. 1986. "Family and social factors associated with substantiation of child abuse and neglect reports." *Journal of Family Violence.* 1(2): 1676-79.

Krishnan, Vijaya and Morrison, Kenneth B. 1994. "An ecological model of child maltreatment in Canadian province. *Child Abuse and Neglect.* 19(1): 101-113.

Lassiter, Ruby F. 1987. "Child rearing in Black families: Child-abusing discipline?" In *Violence in Black families: Correlates and consequences.* 1st edition. ed. R. Hampton, 39-53. Massachusetts: Lexington Books.

Lauderdale, M., Valiunas, A. and Anderson, R. 1980. "Race, ethnicity, and child maltreatment: An empirical analysis." *Child Abuse and Neglect.* 4: 163-69.

Laurer, B., Broeck, E. T. and Grossman, M. 1975. "Battered child syndrome: Review of 130 patients with controls." *Pediatrics.* 53: 67-70.

Leventhal, John M. 1982. "Research strategies and methodologic standards in studies of risk factors for child abuse." *Child Abuse and Neglect.* 6: 113-23.

Levin, Patricia G. 1983. "Teachers' perceptions, attitudes, and reporting of child abuse and neglect." *Child Welfare.* 62(1) (Jan.-Feb.): 14-20.

Light, R. J. "Abuse and neglected children in America: A study of alternative policies." *Harvard Education Review.* 43: 556-98.

Likert, Rensis, and Likert, Jane Gibson. 1976. *New ways of managing conflict.* New York: McGraw Hill Book Company.

Lindsey, Duncan. 1994. *The welfare of children.* New York: Oxford University Press.

Litwak, Eugene and Hylton, Lydia F. 1962. "Interorganizational analysis: A hypothesis on co-ordinating agencies." *Administrative Science Quarterly.* 6: 395-420.

Lobb, Michael L. and Strain, George Michael. 1984. "Temporal patterns of child abuse and neglect reporting: Implications for personnel scheduling." *Child Welfare.* 62(5): 453-64.

Lona, K. A. 1986. "Cultural consideration in the assessment and treatment of intrafamilial abuse." *American Journal of Orthopsychiatry.* 56(1) (January): 131-6.

McCaffrey, M. and Tewey, S. 1978. "Preparing educators to participate in the community response to child abuse and neglect." *Exceptional Children.* 45(2): 114-22.

McCarthy, B. J., R. W. Rochat, B., Cundiff, P. A. Gould and S. Quave. 1981. "The child abuse registry in Georgia: Three years of experience." *Social Medicine.* 74: 11-16.

McDonald, Anne and Reece, Robert. 1979. "Child abuse: Problems of reporting." *Pediatric Clinics of North America.* 26(4): 785-91.

McGee, Robin A., David A. Wolfe, Sandra A. Yue, Susan K. Wilson, and Jean Carnochan. 1995. "The measurement of maltreatment: A comparison of approaches." *Child Abuse and Neglect.* 19(2): 233-249.

McPherson, K. S. and Garcia, L. L. 1983. "Effects of social class and familiarity on pediatricians' responses to child abuse." *Child Welfare.* 62(5) (Sept.-Oct.): 387-93.

Mackrimmon, N. J. 1978. "Role strain: Assessment of a measure and its invariance of factor structure across studies." *Journal of Applied Psychology.* 63(3): 321-28.

Maden, M. 1980. *The dispositionof reported child abuse.* Saratoga, California: Century Twenty-One.

Maidman, Frank. 1984. *Child welfare: A source book of knowledge and practice.* New York: Child Welfare League of America, Inc.

Magura, A. and Moses, B. 1983. *Child maltreatment rating scales*. New York: Child Welfare League of America, Inc.

Manley-Casimir, Michael E. and Newman, Beth. 1976. "Child abuse and the school." *Canadian Welfare*. 52(4): 17-19.

Maryland Department of Human Resources Social Services Administration. 1986. "Child abuse in Maryland: The central registry report 1984." *Publication #1058*. Baltimore, Maryland.

Maryland Department of Human Resources Social Services Administration. 1989. "Child abuse in Maryland-1987." Baltimore, Maryland.

Maryland Family Law Code Annotated Subtitle 7, Regulations: 07.02.07.07. July 1, 1988. Annapolis, Maryland.

Maryland's Civil Abuse and Neglect Law Articles Subtitle 7. October 1, 1994. Annapolis, Maryland.

Mayhill, Pamela D. and Norgard, Katherine G. 1983. *Child abuse and neglect: Sharing responsibility*. New York: John Wiley & Sons.

Merton, Robert K. 1964. "Structural analysis in sociology." In *Approaches to the study of social structure*, ed. Peter Blau, 21-52. New York: The Free Press.

Meddin, Barbara J. 1985a. "The assessment of risk in child abuse and neglect case investigation." *Child Abuse and Neglect*. 9(2): 57-62.

_____. 1985b. The services provided during a child abuse and/or neglect case investigations and the barriers that exist to service provision." *Child Abuse and Neglect*. 9(2): 175-82.

Miles, R. H. 1976. "A comparison of the relative impacts of role perceptions of ambiguity and conflict by role." *Academy of Management Journal*. 19(1): 2535.

Miller, Delbert C. 1977. *Handbook of research design and social measurement*. 3rd. edition. New York: David McKay Company, Inc.

Morris, John L., Johnson, Charles F. and Clasen, Mark. 1985. "To report or not to report: Physicians' attitudes toward discipline and child abuse." *American Journal of Disease of Children*. 139(2): 194-7.

Muehlman, Thomas and Kimmons, Cheryl. 1981. "Psychologists view on child abuse reporting, confidentiality, life, and the law: An exploratory study." *Professional Psychology*. 12(5): 631-38.

Nagi, Saad Z. 1975. "Child abuse and neglect programs: A national overview." *Children Today.* 4 (May-June): 13-17.

————. 1977. *Child maltreatment in the United States: A challenge to social institutions.* New York: Columbia University Press.

Newberger, Eli H. and Bourne, Richard. 1978. "The medicalization and legalization of child abuse." *American Journal of Orthopsychiatry.* 48(4): 593-607.

Nixon, J., J. Pearn, I. Wilkey, and G. Petrie. 1981. Social class and violent child death: An analysis of fatal non-accidental injury, murder, and fatal child neglect." *Child Abuse and Neglect.* 5: 111-16.

Oates, Kim. 1984. *Child abuse: A community concern.* New York: Brunner/Mazsel Publisher.

Park, R., and Collmer, C. 1975. "Child abuse: An interdisciplinary review." In *Review of child development research,* ed. E. M. Hetherington, Chicago: University of Chicago Press.

Pelton, L. H. 1985. "Child abuse and neglect: The myth of classlessness." In *The social context of child abuse and neglect,* ed. L. Pelton, 23-38. New York: Human Sciences Press.

Pierce, Robert and Pierce, Lois H. 1985. "The sexually abused child: A comparison of male and female victims." *Child Abuse and Neglect.* 9: 191-99.

————. 1987. "Child sexual abuse: A Black perspective." In *Violence in Black families: Correlates and consequences.* 1st edition. ed. R. Hampton, 67-85. Massachusetts: Lexington Books.

Polansky, Norman A., Mary Ann Chalmers, Elizabeth Buttenwieser, and David Williams. 1975. "Asssessing adequacy of child caring: An urban scale." *Child Welfare.* 4 (May-June): 1317.

Polier, Justine Wise. 1975. "Professional abuse of chiildren: Responsibility for the delivery of services." *American Journal of Othopsychiatry.* 45(3) (April): 357-362.

Powers, Deb. 1985. "Child abuse: After the report is made." *Wisconsin Medical Journal.* 84(3) (March): 13-15.

Purvine, Margaret, and Ryan, William. 1969. "Into and out of child welfare network." *Child Welfare.* 48 (March): 126-35.

Rabb, Joel A. 1981. "Reporting child maltreatment: The context of decision making among physicians, social workers, teachers, and nurses." Doctoral Dissertation, Ohio State Univerity.

Reinhart, Michael A. 1983. "Reporting suspected child abuse." *Journal of the American Medical Association.* 249(15): 2017.

Reiniger, Anne, Robison, Esther, and McHugh, Margaret.1995. "Mandated training of professionals: A means for improving reporting of suspected child abuse." *Child Abuse and Neglect.* 19(1): 63-69.

Richey, D. Dean. 1980. "Educators and the primary invention of child abuse." *Educational Forum.* XLIV.

Rosen, Helen. 1984. "How workers use cues to determine child abuse." *Social Work Research and Abstracts.* 148 (Winter): 27-33.

Resenfeld, Alvin A. and Newberger, Eli H. 1977. "Compassion-vs-conrtrol: Conceptual and practical pitfalls in the broadened definition of child abuse." *Journal of the American Medical Association.* 237(May): 2086-88.

Saulsbury, Frank T., and Campbell, Robert E. 1985. "Evaluation of child abuse reporting by physicians." *American Journal of Diseases of Children.* 139(4) (April): 393-5.

Schuchter, Arnold. 1976. *Perspective package: Child abuse intervention.* Washington, DC: U.S. Government Printing Office.

Sharwell, G. R. 1978. *Child abuse and neglect: Legislation, reporting, and prevention.* Lexington, Massachusetts: D.C. Heath and Company.

Sheldon, Stephen H. and Levy, Howard B. 1985. "Child abuse reporting. "*American Journal of Disease of Children.* 139(12): 1176-77.

Silverman, F. N. 1953. "The roentgen manifestations of unrecognized skeletal trauma in infant." *American Journal of Roentgenal.* 69: 413-427.

Smith, S. M. and Hanson, R. 1974. "134 battered children: A medical and psychological study." *British Medical Journal.* 3: 660-70.

Starr, R., Beresnie, S. and Rossi, J. 1976. "What child abuse researchers don't tell about chold abuse research." *Pediatric Psychology.* 1: 50-53.

Stein, T. J. 1984. "The child abuse prevention and treatment act." *Social Service Review.* 58(2): 302-14.

Taylor, L. and Newberger, Eli H. 1979. "Child abuse in the international year of the child." *New England Journal of Medicine.* 301: 1205-1212.

Theisen, W. M. 1979. "What's next in child abuse policy? Improving the knowledge base." *Child Welfare.* 57(7): 415-21.

Turbett, J. P. and O'toole, R. "Teachers recognition and reporting of child abuse." *Journal of School Health.* 53(10: 605-9.

Tyler, Ann H. 1984. "Abuse in the investigation and treatment of intrafamilial child sexual abuse." *Child Abuse and Neglect.* 8(1): 47-53.

U.S. Department of Health and Human Services. 1981. "National analysis of official child neglect and abuse reporting." *DHHS Publication No. (OHDS) 80-30271,* Washington, D.C.

_____. 1981. "Study findings: Incidences of severity of child abuse and neglect." *DHHS Publication No. (OHDS) 81-30325.* Washington, D.C.

U.S. Department of Health and Human Services, National Center on Child Abuse and Neglect. 1995. *Child maltreatment 1993: Reports from the states to the national center on child abuse and neglect.* Washington, D. C.: Government Printing Office.

U.S. Department of Health, Education, and Welfare. 1981. *Model child protection act with commentary.* Washington, D. C.

Valentine, D. P., D. S. Acuff, M. L. Freeman, and T. Andreas.1984 "Defining child maltreatment: A multidisciplinary overview." *Child Welfare.* 6 (Nov.-Dec.): 497-509.

Vander Mey, B. J., and Neff, R. L. 1986. *Incest as child abuse: Research and application.* New York: Praeger Publishers.

Weinberger, Paul E. and Smith, Peggy J. 1966. "The disposition of child neglect cases referred by caseworkers to a juvenile court." *Child Welfare.* 43: 457-63.

Wells, Dorothy P. 1980. *Child abuse: An annotated bibliography.* New Jersey: The Scarecrow Press, Inc.

Wooley, P. V. and Evans, W. A. Jr. 1955. "Significance of skeletal lesions in infants resembling those of traumatic origin." *Journal of the American Medical Association.* 158: 539-543.

Young, L. 1964. *Wednesday's child.* New York; McGraw-Hill.

Zuravin, S. J. and Starr, Raymond, H. 1991. "Psychosocial characteristics of mothers of physically abused and neglected children: Do they differ by race?" In *Black family violence: Current research and theory,* ed. R. L. Hampton, 35-70. Massachusetts: Lexington Books.

Zuravin, S. J., Watson, B. and Ehrenschaft, 1987a. M. "Severity of anonymously made reports of child abuse: Policy and program implications." Grant Study supported in part by *National Center on Child Abuse and Neglect Grant 90-CA-0922101*. University of Maryland at Baltimore School of Social Work and Community Planning.

_____. 1987b. "Anonymous reports of child abuse: Are they as serious as reports from other sources." Child Abuse and Neglect. 11: 521-529.

Index